PROPHETS
AND THE
PROPHETIC
MOVEMENT

by
DR. BILL HAMON

foreword by
Dr. Gary Greenwald

CHRISTIAN INTERNATIONAL
Route 2 Box 351
Point Washington, FL 32454
(904) 231-5308

edited by Paul Thigpen

First Printing: 15,000

PROPHETS 2 THE PROPHETIC MOVEMENT
    God's Prophetic Move Today
Copyright © W.S. "Dr. Bill" Hamon, 1990
Printed in the United States of America

Library of Congress: 90-80938

International Standard Book Number:0-939868-04-0 (Vol2)
International Standard Book Number:0-939868-03-2 (Vol1)
International Standard Book Number:0-939868-02-4 (Set)

Produced by
CHRISTIAN INTERNATIONAL MINISTRIES

Published by
DESTINY IMAGE
351 N. Queen Street
Shippensburg,PA 17257-0351

FOREWORD

The prophet is perhaps the most misunderstood of the fivefold ministry in the Church. And the present day Prophetic Movement has the greatest potential for good or evil of any movement in 500 years of Church restoration. Therefore, our generation needs to fully understand God's timeless purpose for prophets and His Prophetic Movement.

I am enthused that a man with Dr. Bill Hamon's qualifications has been used of God to present such a needed understanding on the current purpose of God in His prophets and Prophetic Movement. Dr. Hamon is not a novice in the faith but one with a proven track record of 38 years of fruitful ministry. He envisioned and established the Network of Prophetic Ministries which is now giving oversight to hundreds of prophets and prophetic ministers.

We've heard much about "false prophets" but where are the "true prophets" in the Church today? Dr. Hamon clearly answers this question by giving an insightful overview of the Prophetic Movement.

The supernatural Prophetic Movement is God's standard that He is raising up to expose and overcome the flood of demonic activity in witchcraft, satanic seduction, occultic manipulation and the New Age movement. The powerful words and music of prophetic warfare praise is arising to counteract the satanic music that is influencing many of the younger generation. There has never been a more timely need of the restoration of God's prophets than at this very hour. This volume is a timely "must".

Dr. Gary Greenwald

Senior Pastor - Eagles Nest, Santa Ana, CA
Author of "Seductions Exposed"

iii

DEDICATION

This book, "Prophets-2" is dedicated to all the believers in Christ Jesus who will have "ears to hear" what the Holy Spirit is saying to the corporate Body of Christ; to those who will perceive and receive God's true prophets and co-labor with the Holy Spirit in His great restorational move to activate and establish Christ's ascension gift and fivefold ministry of **Prophet** and the **Prophetic Ministry** fully into His Church.

APPRECIATION

Appreciation is given to my CI-NPM Board of Governors who, by their dedicated ministry and support, made it possible for their Bishop to take the time from his active traveling ministry to fulfill his commission from Christ to stay home and finish this desperately needed book. Heartfelt appreciation is given to my wife, Evelyn, for her encouragement for me to finish the book, and to the CI staff and CI-NPM ministers for carrying on the ministry while their President was writing.

CONTENTS

FOREWORD by Gary Greenwald iii

DEDICATION and APPRECIATION iv

The MAKING of a PROPHET by Leon Walters 1
God's Providential Processes in Natural Circumstances
Romans 8:28—God's Principle for Prophets in Preparation

MOTIVATION and PURPOSE 7
The Spirit and Intent of the Author
The Purpose and Mission of the Book

**1. THE IMPORTANCE OF UNDERSTANDING
THE PROPHETIC MOVEMENT** 11
"Where are the Prophets?"
A Tidal Wave Coming
Prophetic Movement—Greatest Potential For Good or Evil
Believe and Receive God's True Prophets
God Loves His True Prophets
The Logos Has Unique Authority

**2. THE NATURE OF A RESTORATION
MOVEMENT** 19
Apostles and Prophets Are Foundational
Why Some Have Denied Apostles and Prophets
Rejection Results from Reaction rather than Scriptural Realities
"Restoration Movement" Defined
Acts the Pattern for New Testament Church Age
Eight Dispensations, Covenants, Ages
Nine Major and Minor Movements

**3. GOD'S PROVIDENTIAL PREPARATION
AND PRINCIPLES FOR RESTORATION** 25
The Creation of Planet Earth
Man, Message and Methods
Restoration of Abraham's Seed Back to Canaan
Jesus Provided All Things
The Church Is Central to God's Purpose
Prophets Prophesied the Church's Restoration
Fulfillment Before Finality

3. GOD'S PROVIDENTIAL PREPARATION...(Cont.)

Why Hasn't Jesus Come Back?
Prophets Are the Key
Prophetic Evangelism

4. A BRIEF HISTORY OF CHURCH RESTORATION 37

The Seven Doctrines of Christ
FOUR MAJOR RESTORATION MOVEMENTS
   SUMMARIZED
The Historic Protestant Movement
The Holiness/Evangelical Movement
The Classical Pentecostal Movement
The Latter Rain/Charismatic Movement
A Gigantic Final Tidal Wave of Restoration is Coming
The "Snowball" Principle of Restoration
50 Years of Fivefold Restoration
Evangelist-50's;Pastor-60's;Teacher-70's;Prophet-80's;
   Apostle-90's
Men Alive in 1990 Representing 40 Years of Renewal

CHARTS — Restoration and Destiny of Church ... 51

5. CHARISMATIC MOVEMENT COMPARED TO THE PROPHETIC MOVEMENT 55

An End Time Davidic Company
The Charismatic and Prophetic Movements Compared
Wilderness Walkers vs. Canaan Conquerors
Apostolic Cloud and Prophetic Fire
Prophets are Pioneers, Marines, Space Explorers

6. WHAT IS THE PROPHETIC MOVEMENT ALL ABOUT? 59

The Role of Prophets in Restoration
What Does the Prophetic Movement Include?
New Ways to Minister Prophetically
Protestant, Pentecostal and Prophetic "Gift" Restorations
A PERSONAL TESTIMONY
Prophetic Presbytery Customs
A Sovereign Move of God
Training and Activating Others
Spirit of the Prophet Subject to the Prophet
Can You Make God Talk?
The Nabi Prophet
Teaching Others to Minister Prophetically
Proof in the Fruit of the Ministry
The Last Great Harvest Reaped by the Saints

7. SEVEN PRINCIPLES OF A TRUE RESTORATION MOVEMENT 81

Restoration Movement vs. Spiritual Renewal
(1) DIVINE ENLIGHTENMENT AND REVELATION KNOWLEDGE OF THE TRUTH
    Martin Luther and Protestant Movement Establish Principles
    New Applications of Restored Truth
(2) OCCASIONAL INDIVIDUAL VS. CONSISTENT COMPANY
(3) NEW ANOINTING & AUTHORITY FOR ESTABLISHING TRUTH
(4) A SMALL BEGINNING IN AN INSIGNIFICANT PLACE
    Jesus-The-Messiah Movement
    New Testament Church Movement
    Protestant Movement Beginnings
    Birth of the Pentecostal Movement
    The Beginnings of the Prophetic Movement
    The Birth of the Prophetic Movement
    Forty Year Period of Faithful Prophets
    Other Prophetic Ministries
    The Prophets Are God's Great End-Time Sign
(5) POWER TO REPRODUCE BY TEACHING, TRAINING, ACTIVATING AND MATURING THE SAINTS
    The Reproduction Principle
    Protestant Movement Reproducers
    1948 Seed Prophets - 1988 Reproducing Prophets
    A Clarification of Terms
    A Reproducer of Reproducers
    Prophets Training Prophets
(6) PRACTICED AND PUBLICIZED UNTIL CONTESTED AND CONTROVERSIAL
    Past Movement Leaders Oppose the New
    New Race Started Every Two Thousand Years
    All Restoration Churches Are "Ecclesia"
    The Prophetic Movement in the 1990's
(7) NEW SONGS, CHORUSES, AND OTHER MUSIC PORTRAYING THE RESTORATION MESSAGE
    Holiness Movement Songs
    Pentecostal Songs
    Latter Rain Worship
    Charismatic Worship
    A Prophetic Movement Minstrel and Warfare Praise

8. A CRY FOR BALANCE, STRUCTURE AND ORDER 123

    Understanding the Process
    Extreme Swings in the Pendulum of Restored Truth

8. A CRY FOR BALANCE... (Cont.)

The 1500's—Justification by Faith
The 1600's—Water Baptism
The 1700's—Holiness, Sanctification, and Perfectionism
The 1800's—The Second Coming of Jesus
The 1880's—Divine Faith Healing
The 1900's—Holy Ghost Baptism and Other Tongues
The 1940's—Laying on of Hands and Personal Prophecy
The 1950's—Praise-Singing, Body Ministry, Praise-Dancing
The 1960's—Demonology: Oppression, Obsession, or Possession?
The 1970's—Discipleship, Family Life, Church Growth
The 1970's—Faith Message, Prosperity, Word Teaching
The 1980's—Kingdom Now, Dominion, Reconstructionism
The 1990's—Prophets, Prophetic Movement, Prophetic People
Abuses and Extremes in the Use Of Personal Prophecy
The Restoration of Prophets Absolutely Essential
The Restoration Cycle of History
Abuses Have Already Begun
"There Must Also Be Heresies"

9. THE SPIRIT OF TRUE PROPHETS AND THE PROPHETIC MOVEMENT 143

Motivation as Important as Ministry
The Spirit of Wisdom
Joshua Generation Arising
The World's View of a Prophet
Prophets are Real People
Prophets are Powerful Intercessors
Personality of True Prophets
10 M's for Determining True Prophetic Ministers

10. THE PROPHETIC MOVEMENT VS. THE NEW AGE MOVEMENT 157

Real vs. Counterfeit
Discern Through Teaching and Spirit
Common New Age Teachings
Jesus is the Only Way, Truth, and Life

11. GOD'S STANDARD: HIS PROPHETS AND PROPHETIC CHURCH 163

Prophets are God's Standard for Supernatural Communications
God Still Hates False Spirit Communications
Nationwide Televised Confrontation
Religious Witchcraft
The Greatest Indication of Where the Church is

12. WHAT WILL THE ROLE OF THE PROPHETS BE? 169

The Nature of a Prophet
How Does Someone Become a Prophet?
An Apostolic-Prophet
Logos Word vs. Prophet's Rhema Word
Does the Holy Spirit Replace the Prophet?
When and to Whom Personal Prophecy May Be Ministered
Ministerial Ethics Must be the Same for All Ministers
Prophets, Prophecy, and Doctrine
The Church Council at Jerusalem
Five Principles for Establishing Doctrine
The Relationship of Prophets to Other Fivefold Ministers
God's First Order of Establishing the Fivefold
No Perfect Structure Until Apostles Restored

13. PROPHETS POSITIONS AND PRIVILEGES AS ONE OF THE FIVEFOLD MINISTERS 187

Two Prideful Extremes to be Avoided
Five Principles Concerning Fivefold Ministers
Artificial Methods of Determining Ministry
No One Person But Jesus Is All Five
Apostles Used As Examples of All
Personality Profiles for Prophets
Can Prophets Govern and Be Heads of Ministry?
O.T. Prophets Prove That N.T. Prophets Can Govern
Apostles Can Prophesy Guidance, Gifts and Ministries
Modern Day Apostolic-Prophets and Prophetic-Apostles
The Historical Development of "Bishop"
Prophets and Apostles Both Needed

14. THE DIVINE PROCESS IN PROPHETIC FULFILLMENT 209

Noise - Shaking - Coming Together
Muscle and Flesh - Skin - Breath of Life
Army of the Lord - Executing God's Judgment
Restoration to Home Land: Saints Take the Kingdom

15. PROPHETIC CONCLUSION AND CHARGE 217

Timely and Divinely Directed
There is a Restorational Prophetic Movement
Prophetic Charge for Unity
An Appeal to the Apostles
Response to the Prophets Is Critical

15. PROPHETIC CONCLUSION... (Cont.)

Jesus the Prophet Was Rejected
Heroes of the Faith Are Needed Today
Is the Product or Person the Problem?
The Prophet Prepares the Way for Christ to Return
  and Put Satan in the Bottomless Pit
Even so, come, Lord Jesus! Amen.

CAPITALIZATION

Dr. Hamon has taken *Author's Prerogative* in capitalizing certain words which are not usually capitalized according to the standard grammatical practice. This is done for the purpose of clarity and emphasis. Reference to the Church/Bride are capitalized because of Her union with Deity through Jesus Christ. **Prophets** are put in bold in chapter one and a few other places for emphasis. The word Scripture is capitalized only when referring to the whole Bible. Church and Body when referring to the universal Body of Christ the Church; church when referring to a denominational or local church. Logos/Word when referring to the whole Bible; rhema/word when referring to individual scriptures or prophetic words.

All scriptures are taken from King James versions (KJV, NKJV) except when designated. When quoting scripture the author sometimes adds **bold** or *italic* for emphasis.

THE MAKING OF A PROPHET

When God called Jeremiah, he told him: *"Before I formed you in the womb I knew you, and before you were born I consecrated you; I have appointed you a prophet to the nations"* (Jer.1:5). But the making of a prophet involves more than being preordained in Christ and called by God this way. When the Apostle Paul was telling the Ephesians how he became the minister he was, he said, *"I was **made** a minister, according to the gift of God's grace which was given to me according to the working of His power. To me, the very least of all saints, this grace was given"* (Eph.3:7,8). The predestinated calling of a prophet is only the beginning of the process God takes a man through to **make** him into an individual that can handle the burden and pressures of that ministry.

This calling is like being born again—an instantaneous, divine gifting experience. But the progressive preparation, like the process of spiritual growth that follows the initial salvation experience, requires years. Few men ever allow God to take them through everything required to mature them in what could be called the "10 M's of the Proven Minister": Manhood, Message, Ministry, Maturity, Marriage, Motive, Money, Methods, Manners and Morality (see chapter 9).

Bill Hamon is one man who has allowed God to take him through that process to become the proven apostolic prophet minister that he is today. The first prophetic presbytery that ever ministered to him declared that God had called him as He had called the prophet Jeremiah. But God's process had to follow the call.

Dr. Hamon's nearly four decades of teaching and three books can validate the biblical accuracy of his message. His ministry has been proven as he has ministered prophetically to over 20,000 individuals: Many of those prophecies have already come to pass with miracles of healings and divine provision accompanying them.

Thousands can thus validate Dr. Hamon's message and ministry. But few know him as I have had opportunity to know him with regard to the other "M's." Today his family especially stands as a testimony to his character: He and his wife Evelyn have been married more than 35 years; they have three married children and nine grandchildren. All three children with their spouses are working full-time with him in the ministry. This speaks as loudly as his mighty messages and ministry.

My first contact with Bill and Evelyn Hamon was in July, 1962, when they participated in my wedding to Donna, Evelyn's younger sister. My next time to be around Dr. Hamon was when he came to teach at the Bible college where I was finishing my last year. He was only thirty years old at the time but his wisdom, anointing and ability to teach the Word and minister the Holy Spirit to the students was a tremendous blessing. The prophetic insight into the scriptural truth about the Church and God's purpose for this present age which Dr. Hamon demonstrated nearly thirty years ago have proven true over the years, and they are the same truths he is teaching today—except with greater illumination and prophetic application.

After I graduated, I moved to Denver, Colorado, we didn't see each other, except at occasional family get-togethers. But fourteen years later God called me by two angelic visitations to leave my established decorating and contracting business to fulfill my call to the ministry. Dr. Hamon gave me an invitation to work with Christian International, and I gladly accepted.

Through many providential workings, such as the failure of our house to sell for an extended period of time, our two families ended up living together in the same home for five years. Dr. Bill, Evelyn and their children not only had my wife, our three daughters, and me living with them, but also his mother-in-law and—for awhile—two other young people. We had up to thirteen people living in the same house at one time!

You can see, then, that I've had ample opportunity to observe Dr. Hamon's personal life from an intimate perspective. I can honestly say that in those five years of living together, there were no blow-ups between the families, and Bill and Evelyn made all of us feel that it was our home just as much as theirs. This providential situation was no doubt part of God's process in developing the grace and wisdom that Dr. Hamon would need to become an apostolic prophet working with a great family of prophets and prophetic ministers for which he would have the responsibility of oversight and fatherhood.

But that was by no means the toughest part of God's maturing process for Dr. Hamon. In fact, Evelyn is planning to write a book telling in detail about the numerous experiences in their life which illustrate the processes God takes a prophet through to develop the character of Jesus Christ: humility, patience, mercy, wisdom and maturity. But Dr. Hamon himself would identify three other periods of his life—each lasting three years—to be the greatest testing of his faith and making of his manhood. In these three situations, he had *"the rug pulled out from under him"* either by those who were over him or those who were co-laboring with him. Like Joseph and David, Dr. Hamon knows what it's like to go from being *"favored by the father"* to being *"sold into Egypt by the brethren."*

Bill Hamon began pastoring when he was nineteen years old, and enjoyed several years of pastoral ministry. During that time he married and had two sons. He and Evelyn then started traveling in evangelistic ministry, but in 1961 his wife developed complications in the last few months of her third pregnancy. They returned to Yakima Valley in Washington State, where he had pastored and Evelyn's family lived. God worked a miracle to bring the mother and newborn daughter through victoriously.

The next three years Dr. Hamon had no ministerial pulpit position, and he felt as if he were in Egypt. But it was also during this time when God required him to place the greatest ambition of his life on the altar of sacrifice. The full-time ministry was his Isaac, and God had him give it up. His wife says she grew much in grace and wisdom as well during that difficult period.

In 1964 Dr. Hamon was called to be a full-time teacher at the Bible college in San Antonio, Texas. He had five years of enjoyable and fruitful ministry there. Then suddenly, without notice or personal anticipation, he was separated from that ministry and had to go back to secular work to support his family while he was building the Christian International Correspondence Bible College.

During this period, Dr. Hamon felt as if he were like Joseph: going from being governor of the prison with Potiphar to being an inmate in the prison. For anyone who is called to full-time ordained ministry and who has functioned there for years, secular work is like being in prison. During this time God took Dr. Bill through a grace development process in the area of forgiveness. He had to fully forgive those whom he felt had wronged him and cut him off from what he believed to be God's will for his life.

This experience began in 1969 and climaxed with an even greater challenge in 1973. During those three years, many good things happened: Dr. Hamon had brought Christian International from being a vision received and incorporated in 1967 to being an established college with several courses he had written and had directed others to write. In 1970, three extension colleges were started in Topeka, Kansas; San Antonio, Texas; and Mindanao, the Philippines. Then in 1973 a national university granted Bill Hamon an Honorary Doctorate in recognition of his outstanding work in building Christian International into a worldwide ministry to the Body of Christ.

Despite all the positive things happening, however, Dr. Hamon did not understand much about corporate structure in those days. The result was that the president of the board of directors of the college personally decided to close the college because of financial pressure. Meanwhile, the college had been moved from the fifth floor of a building downtown to Bill's garage.

Dr. Hamon suddenly found himself in a difficult place: He was a thirty-eight-year-old married man with three teenage children and no source of income, no money in the bank and no one to turn to but the Lord. He had already arranged an itinerary with many pastors in the northwest and northeast parts of the United States to establish Christian International extension colleges in their churches. But now he had no money, a seemingly defunct college in his garage, and no guarantee of the college ever being reactivated—all the employees had been laid off except one secretary, who volunteered to work without salary.

At this point, Dr. Hamon took a daring step of faith. He decided like the four lepers did in 2 Kings 7 to arise in the midst of his hopeless situation and *"go for it."*

The little church Dr. Hamon attended in San Antonio, Texas—where CI was headquartered at the time—took up a $200 offering for him. At that time a national bus line was offering sixty days of unlimited travel for $149. So during the next six weeks Dr. Hamon traveled over 8,000 miles by bus. He started extension colleges in churches in British Columbia, Canada, Washington, Oregon and California.

It was on this trip that Dr. Hamon experienced the sovereign move of God in his life described in chapter six of this book. So God gave him his greatest spiritual breakthrough during one of the most trying times of his life.

Next Dr. Hamon returned home to San Antonio for one night, then immediately began another three weeks of traveling by bus to Illinois, Ohio, Connecticut, New York, and Georgia, then back to Texas. After that humbling initiation in bus travel, God opened up air transportation. Bill and Evelyn have now flown over one million miles representing Christian International and ministering as prophetic ministers of God.

I assumed the responsibility of the administration of the college while Dr. Hamon traveled and finished writing his first book, *The Eternal Church*. From 1979 to 1982 he had his greatest triumphs and greatest tragedies; his greatest accomplishments up to that time and also the most heartbreaking failures; the greatest additions to his family and the greatest personal loss and dealings of God in his life.

Dr. Hamon and Evelyn's three children were married in 1979, '80, and '81, giving them three more wonderful children by marriage. A fifty-thousand dollar check came to the ministry, enabling CI to make the down payment on desperately needed land and buildings for a new headquarters in Phoenix, Arizona.

Just over a year later, however, all the property was lost. It was the most devastating blow Bill ever experienced—to his faith, his administrative ability, his self-esteem and even his qualification to be a leadership minister. But during this time he continued traveling in ministry, writing the book and ministering at the school of the Holy Spirit he had started.

In those days, when I sometimes saw him utterly discouraged and feeling personally worthless and helpless, he would nevertheless go to church services and prophesy by the hour to others, blessing them with the mind of Christ and a great anointing. Then he would return home with his own challenges of faith remaining the same.

Probably the one word that portrays the man best is perseverance— against all odds and with a daring to do as Abraham did: *"Who against hope believed in hope, that he might become the father of many...."* (Rom.4:18). There were years when it seemed that every prophecy Dr. Hamon had received from others was not coming to pass. He had stood on certain prophecies, for example, that had declared God would meet his need, which he was interpreting to be the need for the $40,000 payment to save the property. But the money didn't come in, and the property was lost.

I heard him say several times during that trial of his faith that if it weren't for the fact that he knew beyond any shadow of a doubt that he was a prophet and that personal prophecy was a true ministry, he would have thrown the whole thing out. The only answer that God would ever give him on the loss of the property was this: *"That was the price I was willing to pay for you to gain the wisdom and maturity I wanted you to have; for I can give you buildings and land overnight, but I cannot grow wisdom and maturity in you without taking you through certain processes."*

God also showed Dr. Hamon how those prophecies concerning his greatest need's being met had indeed come to pass, but not in the sense he had anticipated. As a husbandman in the orchard of the prophetic ministry, his life illustrates the divine principle that the husbandman must be one of the first partakers of the fruit and frustrations of prophetic ministry.

I also saw Dr. Bill take the daring challenge he sensed from the Lord to move the ministry from Arizona to Florida. He had directed the first move across those twelve hundred miles of desert from San Antonio to Arizona in December, 1976, but the almost two-thousand mile move from Arizona to Florida fell my lot to carry out in 1984. That move was to fulfill God's providential purposes, though we weren't aware of all of them at the time.

In churches from Florida to Canada, Dr. Hamon had preached and prophesied for years that the next move of God would start on the east coast of the United States. God had also spoken to him when he started the School of the Holy Spirit that the time would come when a sovereign move of God would take place in one of his prophetic meetings. So he didn't understand at the time how that move of God in his meeting could be part of the move that would begin in the east, since he was having his meetings west of the Mississippi (chapter 7 reveals how this came to pass). Nevertheless, as Dr. Hamon has said, *"God always fulfills the personal prophecies that come over me, but never quite the way, at the time, at the place or with the people that I first assumed he would fulfill them."*

Dr. Hamon started conducting prophets and Holy Spirit seminars at CI's headquarters in the Panhandle of Florida. He is now conducting nine CI-Network of Prophetic Ministries sponsored seminars at our home base each year. He's staying home more than going out. God is fulfilling a prophetic word that was spoken to him in 1979, *"I will place you on acreage ...they shall come to you and no longer will you have to go to them"*—but this prophecy is only one among hundreds that have been spoken over Dr. Hamon and the CI-NPM concerning all that we are now doing and so much more that we are yet to prophetically fulfill.

Dr. Hamon was consecrated as Bishop over CI-NPM in 1989. As a member of the CI-NPM Board of Governors he became my Bishop. Hundreds of prophets and prophetic ministers are being trained by Bishop Hamon and the CI-NPM. I'm grateful for the way God has activated my own spiritual ministry and has launched me as a foundational prophet ministry. And the mantle to prophesy over many people at one time that has been upon Bishop Hamon for all these years is flowing through me as well.

The ministry is real, but it's wonderful to know that this man—the man to whom I'm a co-laborer as well as a natural brother-in-law—is also real. The Word of God declares that you know true or false ministers more by the fruit of their personal lives than by the manifestations of their spiritual ministry. In the business world we had a saying that conveyed the same thought: *"You can know a man under pressure, for he will show his true colors."*

I have seen Bishop Bill Hamon under great pressure many times, and he has remained approachable, reasonable and willing to receive instruction and counsel from both his peers and those under his authority. Those who work with him seek to emulate this same spirit of wisdom and faith that works by love. It's a comfort to know that the minister called to be my bishop-overseer is more than a prophet: he is my friend, my brother and a real man of God.

LEON WALTERS

MOTIVATION AND PURPOSE

The response to my first book in this series, *Prophets and Personal Prophecy:* **God's Prophetic Voice Today**, has been overwhelming and deeply gratifying. Now in its fifth printing, that first volume has sold well over 40,000 copies in just over two years. Christians around the world are evidently hungry to learn about prophetic ministry and to experience it firsthand.

The first book's purpose was to provide believers with guidelines for receiving, understanding and fulfilling personal prophecy. More and more Christians in a number of settings are receiving individual words from God for their lives, yet they have usually had little or no teaching about how to handle those words with care. Therefore, volume 1 sought to provide some instruction in that area. It covered such topics as God's purposes for prophets; the nature of personal prophecy; five instruments of prophetic ministry; biblical sources of prophecy; prophetic terminology; the proper response to personal prophecy; and hindrances to fulfilling personal prophecy.

A large portion of the book was devoted to numerous examples of prophecies from nearly forty years of my own firsthand experience in prophetic ministry. These examples dealt with prophetic words about divine healing; ministries, gifts and callings; romance and marriage; business endeavors and financial prosperity; pregnancies, births and babies; geographic moves and other major life decisions; and life-and-death situations.

My desire in writing both the first volume and this second volume in the series was not to present a long and detailed theological dissertation to prove the validity of prophets in the Church today. That will be done in later volumes when there will be a greater need to answer the critics who will arise to oppose the restoration of prophets and apostles.

Rather than attempting to convince the gainsayers, skeptics and unbelievers, I am writing to those who believe that there are apostles and **prophets** in the Church today. My motivation for writing this volume is akin to that of the Apostle John when he wrote his first epistle to the believers and participants in the "New Testament Church Movement" of which Jesus Christ is both founder and head. John said: "These things I have **written to you who believe** in the name of the Son of God, **that you may know** that you have eternal life, and that **you may continue to believe** in the name of the Son of God" (1Jn.5:13). These things about prophets are being written to you who believe, that you may know that you are participating in something that is truly of God and so that you may continue to believe that Jesus Christ is integrally involved in the restoration, recognition and activation of His prophets within His Church.

In this volume, then, I am taking the time to go into a detailed demonstration, through many biblical proofs and historical principles, that what I would call a **restorational "Prophetic Movement"** is taking place now and will continue to spread throughout the Church and the world. This movement, birthed in the 1980's, will continue to grow to full maturity and manifestation in the 1990's. Those who have experienced prophetic ministry in any of its varied forms need more than the guidelines for receiving personal prophecy offered in volume 1; they also need insights that will help them place the entire Prophetic Movement in the broader context of God's eternal plans for the Church.

The purpose of this book is thus twofold. First, it seeks to **establish the reality and the extent of the prophetic movement**. Second, it seeks to **help all of those who participate in the movement** to understand its history; to derive all the benefits from the truths and spiritual experiences that are a part of the movement; and to receive guidelines and wisdom that they may maintain what they have received with integrity and balance while not losing the power nor purpose of God for this restorational move of the Holy Spirit.

My motivation for writing, then, could also be described by

Luke's description of his reason for writing to Theophilus the history of the "Jesus the Messiah Movement." Luke wrote:

> Many have undertaken to draw up an account of the things that have been fulfilled among us, just as they were handed down to us by those who from the first were eyewitnesses and servants of the Word. Therefore, since I myself have carefully investigated everything from the beginning, it seemed good also to me to write an orderly account...so that you may know the certainty of the things you have been taught (Lk.1:1-4, NIV).

In comparing my motivation for writing to Luke's, I am in no way trying to claim the same level of inspiration as the New Testament writers had. Rather, I am simply trying to show an example of a proper biblical motivation in writing and recording what God has done. Only a false prophet would ever believe or proclaim that what he speaks or writes is or would ever be equivalent to Scripture in inspiration or authority.

My purpose for having "undertaken to draw up an orderly account of the things that have been fulfilled among us" in this Prophetic Movement is to make sure that all who read may understand how it came about and how it relates to God's overall purpose. "Since I myself have carefully investigated everything from the beginning, it seemed good also to me to write an orderly account" concerning the coming forth of God's last-days company of prophets during this Prophetic Movement.

Later books in the series will focus on the training, ministry and personal life of the prophetic minister; others will present a biblical defense for skeptics who doubt the validity of the modern-day prophet, personal prophecy and the Prophetic Movement. In the meantime, I pray that this present volume will meet the needs of those who are anxious to understand God's purposes in today's restorational Prophetic Movement.

1

THE IMPORTANCE OF UNDERSTANDING
THE PROPHETIC MOVEMENT

"Where are the Prophets?" In every quarter of the Church today we hear that question ringing. Not only in Charismatic and Pentecostal churches, but even in the old "mainline" denominations, Christians are experiencing prophetic ministry, acknowledging prophetic ministers and wondering where the Holy Spirit is headed in these closing years of the twentieth century.

God's Restorational Plan. I believe that we are in the midst of a divinely ordained move of God: **the Prophetic Movement**. This movement is founded upon all the truths and spiritual experiences that have been restored to the Church during the last five hundred years of Church restoration. The Prophetic Movement is in fact an extension of the Protestant, Holiness, Pentecostal and Charismatic movements.

Each of these movements had as its purpose the restoration of some particular aspect of the Church. The main purpose of the Prophetic Movement is to restore Christ's ascension gift of the **prophet** into Church ministry and structure as it was originally.

A Tidal Wave Coming. Participants in the Prophetic Movement need to realize that it is not an end in itself, but rather a means to an end. I have no doubt that it is a Holy Spirit inspired restorational movement predestined by God for the fulfilling of His ultimate purpose for His Church and planet earth. But it is not

11

the last restoration movement destined to take place within the Church.

I believe that yet another movement of the Holy Spirit will come to restore the office of the apostle to full position and power in the corporate Body of Christ. Then will come still another movement after that, and finally will appear the mightiest restoration movement ever to take place within the Church or world history.

This final movement will be greater than the accumulation of all the restoration movements over the last five hundred years combined. It will bring about the final fulfillment of all prophecies that have been spoken by all God's **prophets** since the world began. Although we know in these days the world will become more wicked and the antichrist will arise, yet Christ's true Church will still triumph victoriously. The final movement will not only bring Christ's Church to her full maturity and stature as His Bride, but it will continue to sweep across the nations of the world like a giant, thousand-foot tidal wave. The end result will be the literal return of Jesus Christ to set up His kingdom upon the earth.

Saints Take the Kingdom. Then at last "the kingdoms of this world [will] have become the kingdoms of our Lord and His Christ." At that time "the God of heaven shall set up a kingdom which shall never be destroyed: and the kingdom shall not be left to other people, but it shall break in pieces and consume all these kingdoms, and it shall stand for ever....Until the Ancient of days comes, and judgment is given to the saints of the most High; and the time comes that the saints possess the kingdom....The saints of the most High shall take the kingdom and possess the kingdom for ever, even for ever and ever....And the kingdom and dominion, and the greatness of the kingdom under the whole heaven, shall be given to the people of the saints of the most High, whose kingdom is an everlasting kingdom and all dominions shall serve and obey Him!" "And he has made us unto our God kings and priests and we shall reign on [and over] all the earth!" (Rev.11:15; Dan.2:44; 7:18,22,27; Rev.5:10).

In the meantime, if we would understand God's plans and purposes for our generation, we must understand His plans and purposes for the Prophetic Movement.

The Prophets Restored. When Christ ascended upon high He gave five major gifts to the Church, and one of those was **prophets**: "And He Himself gave some to be apostles, some **prophets**, some evangelists, and some pastors and teachers" (Eph.4:11, NKJ). Jesus gave them, and God set them in the Church: "And God hath set some in the Church, first apostles, secondarily **prophets**..." (1Cor.12:28).

The Prophetic Movement has been designed by the Holy Spirit to bring full recognition, restoration and activation of **prophets** and the prophetic ministry. The Church desperately needs a greater understanding of the office of **prophet**. It needs to know the **prophet's** anointing, authority, calling, ministry and purpose; how the **prophet** relates to the other fivefold ministers; and how we can properly respond with a right attitude toward God's **prophets**.

All Need to Participate. Every Christian needs to believe in and know about the dimension of the prophetic ministry—not just a few called to be **prophets**, but **all** believers have a part to play. Everyone in the Church is called to the opportunity to participate in one of three groups: (1) those called to be **prophets**; (2) those ministers not called to be **prophets** who nevertheless are called to become prophetic ministers; and (3) all believers, who are called to move in the supernatural gifts of the Holy Spirit and to become God's prophetic people. The **Prophetic Movement** includes all realms of the prophetic: **prophets**, prophetic ministers, prophetic people, personal prophecy, the prophetic presbytery, gifts of the Holy Spirit, prophetic worship, prophetic song, as well as expressive praise signing and dancing, pageantry and numerous ways of worshiping God in the arts and drama (Eph. 4:11; 1Cor.12:7-11; He.2:3,4).

Prophetic Movement—Greatest Potential For Good or Evil.
Every movement since the beginning of the great restoration
period which began in A.D.1500 has become more powerful
with greater potential for salvation or self-destruction. The
process is like the progressive inventions of warfare weapons,
from gunpowder to single-shot rifles to the multiple-firing Gat-
ling gun to our modern rapid-fire assault weapons; from dyna-
mite and nitroglycerin to atomic and hydrogen bombs and now
to space warfare.

If atomic and laser power were to fall into the hands of
unprincipled, self-centered terrorists, they would have no
scruples about using this power to destroy many lives to further
their own selfish ends. They would use these weapons to intimi-
date, manipulate and control people to build their own dictatorial
kingdom.

The ministry of prophets and prophecy is much the same
way. As the latest and most powerful force and spiritual weapon
of warfare being brought forth in the Church, it has the most
potential for blessing or destruction of any restoration movement
during the last five hundred years. **Prophets** and prophecy have
great power to influence and affect the lives of people. If a
prophet does not have a right spirit and motivation, Christ's
character and biblical principles, he or she has the potential to
control and manipulate people with supernatural knowledge,
visions, revelation and miracles. But if a **prophet** does have the
right spirit and motivation, he or she has great power to influence
people for God toward, unity, obedience, humility and Christ-
likeness.

Prophets and prophetic ministry can bring life or death,
blessing or blasting. Like atomic or laser power, the prophetic
can be used for good or evil. Atomic power can generate light
and heat for a whole city or it can be dropped as a bomb and
destroy the city. Laser power directed in proper timing and
proportions can perform surgery to bring healing or it can be
used as a weapon to destroy. The atom and laser are neither
good nor evil in themselves. It is those who have these forces
under their control that determine the end result of their use.

While **prophets and prophetic ministry are of God** and good in themselves, yet if false **prophets**, wrongly motivated ministers, or immature saints begin to use prophetic ministry wrongly, it can cause great destruction in the lives of many people. That is why there needs to be Schools of the Holy Spirit conducted nationwide and in every local church, especially those who plan to participate in propagating the prophetic.

Of all the fivefold ministries, I believe **prophets** need training in wisdom and proper practice of their ministry the most. For that reason, this volume is being followed immediately with volume 3, *The Prophet and His Ministry*, covering the personal pitfalls to avoid and the directives, proper principles and practices desperately needed for true prophetic ministry. The **prophets** must be made knowledgeable of the many pitfalls they must avoid. It is not enough to fill the car with gas to go; the driver must be given driving instructions and a road map if he or she is to use the vehicle properly and reach the desired destination.

Believe and Receive God's True Prophets. Believe God and be established in the present truth; believe in and receive God's **prophets** and you will prosper and find yourself a friend of God. Our father Abraham was a **prophet**, and he was a friend of God (2Pet.1:12; Gen.20:7; Ja.2:23).

Those who favor God's true **prophets** will find God's favor upon their lives. God set **prophets** in the Church to be active throughout all the Church Age. They have not been dispensationally depleted nor cemented into a nonfunctional foundation, as some have claimed. Rather, they are a vital part of all that God has done and will ever do in His eternal plan for humanity (1Cor.12:28; 2Chr.20:20; Mt.10:41; Lk.11:45-52).

God Loves His True Prophets. God takes special pride and interest in His **prophets**. He makes the emphatic declaration in Scripture, "Do my **prophets** no harm" (1Chr.16:22).

Jesus is very sensitive about His ascension gift **prophets**. To touch one of His **prophets** is to touch the apple of His eye, for they are the "seers" in the Body of Christ. To reject Christ's gift of Himself to the Church as the **prophet** is to reject Christ Jesus. To fail to recognize the **prophets**, or to keep them from speaking, is to refuse God permission to speak and minister in this capacity.

Jesus relates to and identifies with the **prophet** (Rev.19:10). He was the full manifestation of all the fivefold ministers—including the **prophet**—in one human body (Col.2:9). Though He was the Good Shepherd, He never had the opportunity to be the pastor of a local church, as we know it, other than discipling the twelve as they journeyed. Nevertheless, He did continually manifest the ministry of the **prophet** (Mt.21:11; Jn.4:19).

Jesus was a prophet in His mortal ministry on earth. He is continuing that ministry by giving the **prophet** part of His mantle to men and women today. Jesus is still alive and functioning in His Church today as a **prophet**. He loves to communicate with His people and speak directly to them.

Jesus is excited about the restoration of His **prophets**. He knows that the great company of **prophets** arising today will prepare the way for His second coming just as the **prophet** John the Baptist prepared the way for His first coming (Is.40:3; Lk.1:17).

The Logos Has Unique Authority. Of course, I affirm emphatically that the Holy Spirit inspired believers to write, and later He directed others to canonize, sixty-six books to form the Old and New Testaments. These are called Scriptures or the **Logos** Word of God. All these Scriptures were given by the inspiration of God, and they are profitable for doctrine, for reproof, for correction, and for instruction in righteousness, so that every believer may become a man or woman of God completely knowledgeable and thoroughly equipped for every good work in Christ Jesus (2Tim.3:16).

The Holy Scriptures are complete; no later writings or prophecies are to be added to, or made an equal to, the Logos Scriptures. Jesus and the Holy Spirit are inseparably one. So He will never speak anything contrary to what is in the written Logos by the inspiration of the Holy Spirit (1Jn.5:7; 2Pet.1:21).

But Jesus still wants to testify in the midst of His Church. He does this through the spirit of prophecy: "For the testimony of Jesus is the spirit of prophecy" (Rev.19:10). The work of the Holy Spirit has not replaced the personal ministry of Jesus speaking a personal, living, present-day, specific **rhema** word to His Church through His **prophets** and **prophet**ic ministry.

Co-Laborers With Christ. Jesus earnestly desires the full restoration of His prophets and the prophetic ministry, for it gives Him greater opportunities to express Himself more fully and specifically to the Church and to the world. All that heaven has to offer is personally co-laboring with Christ to bring His **prophets** to full recognition, position and ministry within the Church and to the world.

You and I also have the opportunity to be co-laborers with Christ in fulfilling His desire (Mk.16:20; 1Cor.3:9; 1Sam.14:45; 2Cor.6:1; Rom.8:17), or we can become a hindrance to His will and purpose for His **prophets**. We have the choice to participate or persecute, to partake or passively ignore what Christ is purposefully doing. As for me and my house, we choose to accept God's restoration of **prophets**, become **prophetic ministers**, and help members of **Christ's Church** become **God's prophetic people.**

2

THE NATURE OF A RESTORATION MOVEMENT

The Holy Spirit is activating a restoration movement today within the corporate Church of Jesus Christ. The purpose of this movement is to **restore** Christ's ascension gift ministry of the **prophet.** To **restore** means to reactivate and reestablish something back to its original state and purpose.

Apostles and Prophets Are Foundational. God set prophets in the Church when it was originally established. The Church is a spiritual building of which Christ is the Chief Corner Stone (1Pet.2:4-6), and the apostle and prophet ministries are the foundation stones of that building (Eph.2:20). God has set apostles and prophets in the Church. They were the most prominent ministers who functioned purposefully and powerfully in the book of Acts. They were ordained by God to continue their function as long as the mortal Church is active on planet earth. Jesus gave prophets to the Church, and there is no record in Scripture of any plans on God's part to recall them or cancel their commission. Jesus Christ is the same yesterday, today and forever (He.13:8).

Why Some Have Denied Apostles and Prophets. So if God has not changed anything, then why do prophets need to be restored? Because false religious leaders and teachers deleted the truth and perverted supernatural practices until the Body of Christ deteriorated from the pattern, principles and practices of the first-century Church. By the fifth century the Church of Jesus had fallen away, and descended into a thousand years of what historians have called "the Dark Ages."

Reasons Why Some Deny. We will probably never know all the reasons why so many Christian teachers, over the centuries, came to deny that apostles and prophets still function in the Church. Some Christians based their argument for the reliability of Scripture on its apostolic origins; that is, they claimed that we could trust the authority of New Testament Scripture because each book was either written by an apostle or with the sanction of an apostle. For these Christians, then, to speak of modern day apostles seemed tantamount to claiming that certain individuals today could write new Scripture with the same authority as the New Testament writers. They consequently rejected the notion of apostles in the Church today, and they rejected the idea of modern day prophets for similar reasons.

Of course, every responsible participant in the current Prophetic Movement would insist that the authority of the individuals who were inspired to write the Scriptures was a unique authority, and that the words of contemporary prophets and apostles are not equal to the Scriptures. To call someone an apostle or prophet is not to claim that his or her speech is divinely ordained to be infallible. It is rather the recognition that God still has apostolic and prophetic work to do in the Church and the world today which can only be accomplished by the offices of the apostle and the prophet as they are biblically described. The misunderstanding comes from a difference in defining the roles of those two offices.

Rejection Results from Reaction rather than Scriptural Realities. Perhaps another reason some Christians denied the existence of modern day prophets and apostles was that these titles were used at times by individuals whose authority they rejected. Protestants in particular were disturbed by the Catholic church's claim that the Pope was a modern apostle who received his unique authority by "apostolic succession", that is, by the passing on of the Apostle Peter's authority down the generations through an unbroken chain of Roman bishops who succeeded him. Their reaction was not only to deny the existence of an apostolic succession, but to deny as well even the very existence of any apostles at all after the first generation of the Church.

Others reacted to the fact that the title "prophet" has been assumed by a number of heretical and non-Christian leaders throughout history, including Mohammed, the founder of Islam. Perhaps the most famous such self-proclaimed "prophet" in America was Joseph Smith, who established the Mormon cult. The activities of Smith and others may very well have led to the reaction of ultra-dispensationalists in the 1800's, who denied emphatically that apostles, prophets, or even the supernatural gifts of the Spirit were active in the Church today.

Dispensationalist churches typically taught instead that the gifts had ceased with the early Church. They claimed that apostles and prophets were used to lay the foundation for the Church Age, and that these two offices were then cemented into an original foundation ministry without a need for continuation of that ministry. Because so many Christians today have been influenced, especially by dispensational thinking, the Church has a desperate need for scriptural teaching that restores the prophets and apostles back to the original position, power and purpose that God ordained for them in His Church.

"Restoration Movement" Defined. The phrase **restoration movement** is used by church historians and theologians to describe a time when the Holy Spirit acts sovereignly within the Church to restore a biblical truth or ministry back to its proper order and function. The **Prophetic Movement** is God's time for Christ to restore His ascension gift of **prophet** back into His Church, part of the "times of restoration" prophesied by Peter in Acts 3:21. The Holy Spirit has been commissioned to activate and propagate the prophetic ministry within the Church. The Prophetic Movement is a God-ordained movement just like other movements which have taken place within the Church over the last five hundred years.

Acts is the Pattern for the New Testament Church Age. All the truths, ministries, doctrines and supernatural manifestations that were in the early Church as portrayed in the book of Acts were to continue throughout the Church Age. This was the New Covenant that God made with the Church the same as circumcision was the covenant God made with Abraham.

The Law and Tabernacle provided God's Covenant for proper relationship with Him from the time of Moses on Mount Sinai until the time of Jesus on the cross. By His death, burial and resurrection Jesus fulfilled the Law and the Old Covenant, and ushered in a New Covenant, which is identified as the New Testament in the Holy Bible. Prophets and the prophetic ministry were given a continuing position and ministry within the New Testament Church (Gen.17:10; Ex.20:1-26; Lk.22:20).

Dispensations Defined. An explanation of the notion of "times" might be helpful here. Theologians have divided human existence on earth into different periods of time called "dispensations," "covenants" or "ages." These are normally synonymous terms.

A **dispensation** is a period of time during which God works with humankind according to a set of divine rules and principles which humankind must follow in order to have fellowship with God and to fulfill His will. The pattern of God's plan and purpose for that generation is established at the beginning of the dispensation and continues to be God's will and way for humanity until He changes the pattern, after which another dispensation, covenant or age is established.

These are the most commonly accepted designations for the various dispensations, covenants and ages or periods of time which they cover:

DISPENSATION	COVENANT	PERIOD OF TIME (rounded off)
Innocence	Edenic	From the creation to the fall of humankind (Eternity Past)
Conscience	Adamic	From the fall of humankind to the Deluge (1500 years)

DISPENSATION	COVENANT	PERIOD OF TIME (rounded off)
Human Government	Noahic	From the Deluge to the call of Abraham (500 years)
Promise	Abrahamic	From Abraham to the giving of the Law at Mount Sinai (500 years)
Law	Mosaic	From Mount Sinai to the coming of Christ as Messiah (1500 years)
Grace	Church	From Pentecost to Christ's Second Coming (2000 years)
Millennial	Kingdom	From the beginning to the end of the Millennium (1000 years)
Universal	Everlasting	From the end of the Millennium into eternity (Eternity Future)

Within each of these ages are shorter periods of time referred to as times, seasons, years and last days, as well as times of revival or renewal and restoration movements. The Church Age includes the early days of the Church; the great falling away and the Dark Ages; the times of the restoration movements; and the last days and end times. This book will deal primarily with the times of the restoration movements.

Four Major Movements. Church historians recognize the year 1517 as the official beginning of the period of Church restoration. There have been four major movements since that time: the Protestant, Holiness, Pentecostal and Charismatic Movements. The Holiness Movement actually covered a three-hundred-year period and included three truths and Christian practices that were restored. The Charismatic renewal has included three distinct truths that were restored by different movements within the renewal. If we categorize these individual movements according to the particular century and decade when each truth and ministry was restored, it looks this way:

YEAR	RESTORATION MOVEMENT	MAJOR TRUTH RESTORED
1500	Protestant Movement	Salvation by grace through faith (Eph. 2:8,9)
1600	Puritan Movement	Water baptism, separation of Church and state
1700	Holiness Movement	Sanctification, the Church set apart from the world
1800	Faith Healing Movement	Divine healing for the physical body
1900	Pentecostal Movement	Holy Spirit baptism and speaking in tongues
1950	Latter Rain Movement	Prophetic presbytery, praise and worship
1960	Charismatic Movement	Renewal of all restored truth
1970	Faith Movement	Faith confessions, prosperity
1980	Prophetic Movement	Prophets and the gifts of the Holy Spirit

3

GOD'S PROVIDENTIAL PREPARATION
AND PRINCIPLES FOR RESTORATION

Over five hundred years of recorded church history of restoration movements has provided proof of the consistent methods that God the Father directs the Holy Spirit to use in restoring Christ's Church to the place of purity and maturity for presentation as a proper Bride to Jesus Christ the Bridegroom. When God gets ready to do something new, He makes preparation in certain areas. He prepares a **people**, a **product**, and a **place** to perpetuate His plan. The Lord Jesus then raises up a **man** with a **message** and a **ministry** which produces a **movement** that further fulfills His will by various **methods** and **means**.

This is evidenced in the restoration of earth and the creation of humankind, bringing forth the nation of Israel and the coming of the Messiah to establish the Church. Please take note of the key words **people**, **places**, **products** and **man**, **message**, **methods**.

The Creation of Planet Earth. In eternity past when God was ready to activate into reality His "eternal purpose which He purposed in Christ Jesus" (Eph.3:11), He made ready a **place**, planet earth. He then created Adam and Eve to bring forth His **people**. The **product** that was to be used to preserve, propagate and maintain His plan was all of earth's creatures, elements and atmosphere (Gen.1:1-28).

Man—Message—Methods. In God's movement to restore the world back to a right state by removing the wickedness of

25

humanity by a flood, Noah was the **man**. Repentance was his **message**. The ark was the provision for their preservation. Water was the **method** by which the wicked were taken away. The **place** of the ark's preservation was on top of the water until planet earth was ready for the migration of humankind again (Gen.6:13,18; 7:4; 8:4).

Restoration of Abraham's Seed Back to Canaan. When God was ready to deliver Abraham's descendants, who had moved down into Egypt when Joseph brought Jacob and the other sons of Israel into that country, He made the same preparation and followed the same principles. Moses was His **man**. Deliverance was his **message**—"Let My people go, Pharaoh!"

The children of Israel were the **people**. God's **product** to make the **message** work was miracles in nature against the opposition. The **place** to come out of was Egypt, but the **place** of their destiny was **Canaan**, not just freedom and miraculous provision in the wilderness. That was all a means to an end: "He brought us *out* that He might bring us *in* to give us the *land* He sware unto our fathers" (Deut.6:23; Ex.5:1; 6:3,4).

The Restoration of Humanity to God and the Establishment of the Church. The **man** Christ Jesus was the person God provided to bring the redemption and restoration of humankind. Jesus came and died on the cross, giving His life's blood to save humanity from its sins. But bringing humanity out of sin was not an end in itself. It was a means to an end.

Jesus brings people out of Satan's sin-bondage to make them members of His **Church**. Christ's redemptive purpose was to produce a **people** who would be the **people** of God called the **Church**. If you do not understand that God's eternal purposes revolve around Jesus Christ and His Church, then you will never grasp the need and purpose for Church restoration.

Jesus Will Work Through His Church. Everything Jesus will ever do from the day of Pentecost to the endless eternities will be done with His Church. He is the Head and the Church is the

Body of a single unity. This corporate Body is God's chosen instrument for executing all of His eternal purposes.

Jesus loved the Church and gave Himself for her. Jesus purchased the Church with His own blood. The death of Jesus on the cross paid the redemptive price for every person who would become a member of the Church. The resurrection of Jesus authorized the bringing forth of the Church, and the coming of the Holy Spirit on the day of Pentecost gave birth to the Church. (Acts 20:28; Eph.5:25-27; Eph.2:13-16; Col.1:18-29; 1Pet.1:18,19).

Jesus provided **all things** for the birth, growth and maturity of His Church (Jn.17:4; 19:30). He planned, purchased, produced and empowered it. He made **methods, means** and **provisions** for its **perfection** and **presentation** to Himself as a glorious Bride without spot, wrinkle, or blemish, perfect in purity and maturity.

The **product** that paid the price for sinful human beings to become saintly members of Christ's Church was the precious blood of Jesus. The **message** that Jesus preached was "you must be born again...for **I AM** the only way, truth and life...repent...the kingdom of God is at hand" (Jn.3:3; 14:6; Mk.1:15). The Church is the spiritual kingdom of God, the **place** where King Jesus has His domain. The Church is God's dwelling place and head-quarters on earth: Christ's corporate Body for the physical expression and extension of Himself to humankind. The **product** that made the **message** of Jesus as the Messiah believable was the miracles, signs and wonders He performed.

The Church Is Central to God's Purpose. Through Christ's death, burial, resurrection, ascension and sending of the Holy Spirit, the Church was brought forth and established as a central part of God's eternal purposes. The **Church Age** is a **dispensation** and continuing **covenant** which God made with the **mortal Church**. From the typology of the dimensions of the Holy Place in the Tabernacle we find that the Church Age is destined to last about two thousand years.

Everything that was established in the Church is to remain functional until the mortal Church is immortalized into the eternal Church. Then members of the eternal Church will become co-laborers with God to administer His affairs and execute His eternal purposes as they sit together with Christ Jesus on His Father's throne (Rev.2:26,27; 3:21; 1Cor.3:9).

God's Provision for the Church. The saints of the Church have been cleansed by the blood of Jesus and called by the name of Christ (Christ-ian). They have been covered by the robe of righteousness, the garment of praise for their clothing and the Christian armor for their protection. The Word of God is their sword of the Spirit for warfare in the name of Jesus Christ. The gifts of the Holy Spirit are their weapons of warfare (Jn.1:7; Mk.1:17; Is.61:3,10; Eph.6:10-18; 1Cor.12:7-11; 2Cor.10:4,5).

The fruit of the Holy Spirit is the preserving ability that makes them the salt of the earth and brings conformity to the image of Jesus Christ. The fivefold ministry of apostles, prophets, evangelists, pastors and teachers were given by Christ as an extension of His headship ministry to perfect, equip and mature the members of the Church to Christ's full stature and maturity. All of these products, provisions and principles were established as the pattern and purpose of God in the beginning of the Church and were ordained to continue throughout the age of the mortal Church (Gal.5:22-27).

Prophets Prophesied the Church's Period of Great Restoration. Numerous prophetic scriptures from prophets since ancient times speak of restoration. Apostle Peter and Apostle Paul by the spirit of revelation in the knowledge of Christ's purposes declared that these prophets were speaking of Christ's coming as Messiah. They also applied these prophecies to the Church (Eph.1:17-23; 3:1-11).

These men spoke of the falling away of the Church and then the "times of restoration" that would follow. These restoration movements would continue until all things were restored back into the Church and it was brought to the maturity that God requires before Christ can return for His Bride.

Peter's Prophecy. The key scripture for Church restoration comes from Apostle Peter's prophetic presentation in Acts 3. Peter and John had healed the lame man at the gate of the temple. That caused all the Jewish people to gather around Peter and John at Solomon's Porch.

He prophetically preached to them that their Messiah had already come, but their religious leaders had rejected Jesus and caused Him to be crucified. Nevertheless, this Jesus of Nazareth was indeed the Messiah, and this had been confirmed—both by His resurrection and by their healing of this man by the name of Jesus and power of the Holy Spirit.

Times of Restoration. Peter gave his concluding statement concerning Jesus being the promised Messiah with these words in verse 18: "But those things, which God before had shown **by the mouth of all his prophets**, that Christ should suffer, **he hath so fulfilled**". Then he began preaching about the present and prophesying about the future.

> Repent you therefore, and be converted, that your sins may be blotted out, when the **times of refreshing** shall come from the presence of the Lord. And he shall send Jesus Christ, which before was preached unto you: Whom the **heaven must receive until the times of restitution** of all things, which God hath spoken by the mouth of all **his holy prophets** since the world began. And it shall come to pass, that every soul, which will not hear that **prophet**, shall be destroyed from among the people. Yea, and all the **prophets** from Samuel and those that follow after, as many as have spoken, have likewise foretold of these days. Ye are the children of the **prophets**, and of the covenant which God made with our fathers, saying unto Abraham, And in thy seed shall all the kindreds of the earth be blessed (Acts 3:19-21; 23-25).

Note that Peter declared in verses 19 and 20 that the **"times of restoration"** (or restitution or refreshing) will come first, before

Christ Jesus returns again. Then in verse 21 he prophesied that "heaven" is the place that received Christ when He arose from the dead, and it is the place where He will stay until all the "times of restoration" have transpired which God has spoken by the mouth of all His holy prophets since the world began.

Other translations of verse 21 read this way: "Christ must be kept in heaven till the **period of the great restoration**" (Moffatt). "Christ **must** remain in heaven until the final recovery of all things from sin, as prophesied from ancient times" (Living Bible). "Christ Jesus, Whom heaven must receive (and retain) until the time for the complete restoration of all that God spoke by the mouth of all His holy prophets" (Amplified).

Of all the numerous commentaries I have researched, the following comments, I believe, give the most accurate and balanced exposition of Acts 3:21:

(21) Whom the heaven must receive. The words have a pregnant force; "must receive and keep." Until the times of restitution of all things. The "times" seem distinguished from the "seasons" as more permanent. This is the only passage in which the word translated "restitution" in found in the New Testament. Etymologically, it conveys the thought of restoration to an earlier and better state, rather than that of simple consummation or completion, which the immediate context seems, in some measure, to suggest. It finds an interesting parallel in the "new heavens and new earth"—involving, as they do, a restoration of all things to their true order—of 2Peter 3:13. It does not necessarily involve, as some have thought, the final salvation of all men, but it does suggest a state in which "righteousness" and not "sin" shall have dominion over a redeemed and new-created world; and that idea suggests a wider scope as to the possibilities of growth in wisdom and holiness, or even of repentance and conversion, in the unseen world than that which Christendom has too often been content. The corresponding verb is found in the words, "Elias

[Elijah] truly shall **come first** and **restore** all things" (Charles John Ellicot, gen. ed., **Ellicot's Commentary on the Whole Bible**, Grand Rapids, Michigan: Zondervan, 1954, vol. 7, **The Acts of the Apostles**, E. H. Plumtree, p. 19, emphasis added).

John the Baptist was the prophet who came in the spirit of Elijah to prepare the way for the Messiah. It is the **company of prophets** who will equip the Church in the spirit and power of Elijah to prepare the way for the second coming of Jesus as King (Mal.4:5; Mt.11:7,15).

Fulfillment Before Finality. A particular principle manifested throughout Scripture and nature reveals that certain events cannot happen until there is a progressive fulfillment of other things which allow, enable, or make it possible for that event to take place.

In nature we find that fruitful crops cannot be harvested **until** the process of planting, growing and maturing has been fulfilled. A woman cannot become pregnant **until** conception has taken place. And she cannot give natural birth **until** the times of development and labor pains have been fulfilled (Mk.4:26-29).

This same principle is revealed in the Bible. It especially applies to the first coming of Jesus as Messiah and His second coming at the end of the Church Age. One word reveals this principle more than others. Whoever has any doubts about this principle has only to make a biblical study of the word "until."

God's Appointed Time. Christ was held in the heavens for four thousand years before He was allowed to come to the earth as redeemer of humankind, "but when the **fullness of time** was come God sent forth his Son" (Gal.4:4). Christ Jesus was kept in heaven **until** the time appointed by the Father. The terms "appointed time" and "fullness of time" do not mean just an arbitrary date God picked out of nowhere. The "time" is when everything is properly fulfilled and ready for an event to take place.

Many prophecies concerning nations, peoples and places had to be fulfilled and placed in proper order for the coming of the Messiah. Jesus came from the Father, but there were many prophetic scriptures that He had to fulfill before he could ascend back to the Father. He had many Messianic prophecies to live out.

There were prophecies that talked about His place of birth, ministry, suffering, death, burial and resurrection. His greatest enemies could not take Him or kill Him until he had fulfilled these scriptures. The Apostle Peter declared by divine inspiration that all those Messianic Scriptures in the Old Testament **"Christ...hath so fulfilled"** (Acts 3:18).

Volumes have been written on the proofs of Jesus as the promised Messiah. In fact, Jesus fulfilled fifty-nine Messianic prophecies. And we should note especially that Jesus fulfilled more of these prophecies concerning His life, death and resurrection in His last few days than He did in all the rest of His life. Likewise, the Church will fulfill more scripture in the last generation of the mortal Church than has been fulfilled during the last nineteen centuries.

Prophecies About the Church Must Be Fulfilled. Just as Jesus could not ascend **back** to the Father in heaven **until** certain things had been fulfilled, even now He cannot descend from heaven **back** to earth **until** the Church fulfills certain things. Certain prophecies given by the prophets in the Old Testament and by Jesus, the apostles and the prophets in the New Testament must be fulfilled before the event called the **second coming of Christ** can take place.

The scriptures emphatically declare this reality in several places. For example, when Jesus arose from the dead and established the Church, He sat down at the right hand of the Majesty on High at His Father's command. He was to stay in that position for a specified time: "Sit on My right hand **until** I make thine enemies thy footstool" (He.1:13).

Peter said of Jesus: "Whom the heaven must receive **until** the times of restitution of all things spoken by the prophets" (Acts 3:21). The fivefold ascension gift ministers must function **until** every member is ministering and the Church has become a perfect man, even to the fullness of the maturity of Christ (Eph.4:8-15). "Jerusalem shall be trodden down by the Gentiles **until**" and "blindness in part is happened to Israel **until** the fullness of the Gentiles be come in" (Lk.21:24; Rom.11:25).

Why Hasn't Jesus Come Back? Though Christ's greatest desire is to return to earth so He can resurrect and translate His Church into immortality and oneness with Himself, yet He cannot do so until certain things are fulfilled to bring His Bride to the fullness of purity and maturity that the Father has predetermined. Some Christians have asked a question that needs an answer: Since Christ Jesus is Almighty and can do as He pleases, and if He really wants to come back so much, then why doesn't He? Why didn't His "imminent return" take place in the first or second century of the Church?

By that time millions of Christians had been martyred and multimillions were still alive on earth. The gospel had gone to every creature under the sun (Col.1:23). The Church was demonstrating all the power and principles recorded in the book of Acts. And they were a New Testament apostolic church with miracles and mighty ministry. So why didn't Christ return at that time?

There are answers to all these questions. But let it suffice to say here that there seems to be a certain number of Church members Christ needs in order to make up the eternal Body He desires. And those overcoming members who will rule and reign with Him must come to a certain place of maturity and ministry.

Evidently quantity, quality, accomplishments and fulfillment of certain predestinated purposes for the nations of the world, Israel and the Church are involved. The world's cup of iniquity must reach its fullness, even as the sin of the Amorites had to become full before Abraham's descendants could possess

Canaan (Gen.15:16). God's promises that He swore with an oath to Abraham concerning natural Israel and the land of Palestine must be fulfilled.

Prophets Are the Key. But the key to fulfillment of prophecies concerning Israel and the world is the restoration of the Church and the fulfillment of the prophecies concerning it. And the **company of prophets is the key** that God has inserted into the lock of the Church to open up new revelation of the times for truth restoration and fulfillment in the Church (Amos 3:7; Lk.6:22; 11:47-52; Eph.3:5).

Surprisingly, some ministers have a difficult time with this divine principle. If Christians don't believe that the Church must fulfill certain scriptures and accomplish particular purposes—and if they don't believe that the Church has a progressive destiny to be, become and do something before Christ can return—then their main motivation is to try to save as many from hell as possible, and to just maintain salvation enough to make it to heaven themselves by 'enduring to the end' until death or the coming of Jesus takes them out of this wicked world.

The Joshua Generation. When Christians receive a revelation and vision of Christ's restorational purpose and the things that the Church is to accomplish before Jesus returns, that reality stirs up faith and the zeal of the Lord with a militant spirit to leave the wilderness, cross over Jordan and drive out all of the "ites" from the promised land that God has promised the Church. The Church has as great a commission and predestined purpose as Israel to possess and occupy till Jesus comes (Lk.19:13).

Prophetic Evangelism. This term "occupy" implies more than a passive resistance. It refers to a militant occupying force enforcing the rule of the conquering king. As the Church is energized by a new prophetic zeal, we will not only see an increased vision for the evangelization of the world by sending prophets to the nations, but we will hear a greater cry of the Spirit to see the

Church matured, purified and brought to a "perfect man" (Eph.4:13).

Prophetic evangelism will reveal the secrets of human hearts and cause people to fall down and worship God and testify of His mighty works (1Cor.14:24,25). And as in the days of Daniel, through the ministry of the prophet, whole nations will be turned toward God and will receive a testimony of His power (Dan.4:1-37). The prophetic and apostolic voice being added to the Church will begin to intensify both world evangelization and His perfecting work within His Church which will prepare us to go in and take our promised possession.

When the Church has put under its feet all enemies of Christ that He has ordained for them to subdue, then Christ can be released from heaven to return as the manifest head of His physically resurrected and translated Church. Jesus has provisionally put all things under His feet. The feet are in the body, not the head. The Church is His Body, so He has put all things under **our** feet.

Now is the time for the Church to start walking with those conquering feet as the "Joshua Generation." And just as the promise was given to Joshua, so will it be with the prophetic generation: "Every place that the sole of your foot shall tread upon, that I have given unto you...saith the Lord" (Josh.1:3).

4

A BRIEF HISTORY OF CHURCH RESTORATION

Hundreds of Christian denominations, organizations and independent church groups exist within mainline Christendom. Based on their involvement in Church restoration and their doctrines and practices, they can be divided into five major categories: (1) Catholic/Orthodox; (2) Historic Protestant; (3) Holiness/Evangelical; (4) Classical Pentecostal; and (5) Latter Rain/Charismatic. (The following historical summary of these groups is taken from my study of Church history entitled *The Eternal Church*.)

The Catholic and Orthodox Churches maintained the Christian faith during the Dark Ages against the onslaught of pagan barbarianism and Mohammed's fanatical religion, Islam. But they were not a part of the great restoration of the Church. The Protestant Movement formed the beginning of Church Restoration.

Four Major Movements. All Christians who have received God's present truth accept the last four groups—Protestant, Holiness/Evangelical, Classical Pentecostal and Latter Rain/Charismatic—as movements that were Holy Spirit-directed and established by God. They are called major movements because each one restored one of the seven doctrines of Christ listed in Hebrews 6:1,2:

> Therefore leaving the principles of the doctrine of Christ, let us go on to perfection; not laying again the foundation of *repentance from dead works,* and of *faith*

toward God, of the *doctrine of baptisms*, and of *laying on of hands*, and of *resurrection of the dead*, and of *eternal judgment.*

The Seven Doctrines of Christ. The doctrines listed here—repentance from dead works, faith toward God, doctrine of baptisms, laying on of hands, resurrection of the dead and eternal judgment—are taken to apply not only to individual believers but also to the process of restoration in the corporate Church.

When the first six doctrines are restored, then the seventh one, ultimate perfection, can be restored. Doctrines number five, the resurrection of the dead, and number six, eternal judgment, will produce a Church restoration movement before the general resurrection and great white throne of eternal judgment. All other movements of the Holy Spirit to restore certain ministries, minor truths, the fivefold ministers, worship and praise —as well as the renewals of restored truth—are also truly restoration movements. But they are not called major restoration movements because they do not restore one of the seven doctrines of Christ. Thus, the prophetic restoration movement and even the coming apostolic movement are minor restoration movements which will be preparatory in bringing about the restoration of doctrines number five and six, resulting in number seven.

DOCTRINE OF CHRIST	APPROXIMATE DATE	MAJOR RESTORATION MOVEMENT
1. Repentance from dead works	1500	Historic Protestant
2. Faith toward God	1800	Holiness/Evangelical
3. Doctrine of Baptisms	1900	Classical Pentecostal
4. Laying on of Hands	1950	Latter Rain/Charismatic
5. Resurrection of Dead	?	?
6. Eternal Judgment	?	?
7. Ultimate Perfection	?	?

THE FOUR MAJOR RESTORATION MOVEMENTS SUMMARIZED

The Historic Protestant Movement. Three national church denominations were established in the Protestant Movement: the Lutheran in Germany; the Presbyterian in Scotland; and the Anglican in England (called Episcopalian in America).

Historically, the Protestant churches came into existence because Martin Luther, John Knox, Thomas Cranmer and numerous other ministers broke away from the Catholic church, fighting for and establishing the right to be churches separate from Catholicism.

Spiritually, the movement came into existence because a man of God received a revelation of truth that made it impossible for him to continue in the same religious system which he believed was contrary to the Word of God. Luther would have had to deny his knowledge of the Word of God, his conscience and his newly received spiritual experience in order to remain a priest who promoted the doctrines and practices of the Catholic church.

Restorationally, Protestantism came into existence because the Holy Spirit initiated the period of the restoration of the Church. The Protestant churches brought back into the Church the revelation, proper application and reestablishment of the first doctrine of Christ—**repentance from dead works**.

The movement's **purpose** was to activate the period of the great restoration of the Church. Europe was the **place** of its birth and growth. The priests and **people** that came out of the Catholic church were the ones that propagated the movement. The newly invented **product** that publicized its restorational truths was the printing press.

The key **man** God used was Martin Luther. The **message** was repentance from dead works—the teaching that we are justified by the mercy and grace of Jesus Christ through faith, and nothing else. The **ministry** was the preaching of the Word. The **method** was by faith in God and by the use of every means available. The **result** was the corporate Body of Christ, His Church, awakened from her lethargy and apostasy, taking the first of seven steps to ultimate perfection.

The Holiness/Evangelical Movement. This movement's **purpose** was to restore to the eternal Church of Christ—**faith toward God**. It was conceived in Europe, but America became the **place** of its birth and growth to maturity. The **men** God used were numerous; John Wesley is perhaps the man most noted for promoting holiness. The **people** who participated and the ministers who propagated the truth came from Protestant Movement churches.

The **message** was threefold: believer's baptism by immersion, sanctification and divine healing. The **ministry** was the preaching of the Word accompanied by special singers, great conviction, blessing and emotional manifestations and physical healings. The new **products** that carried the message to the ends of the earth were the steamship and railroad.

The **result** was that the eternal Church crossed its Red Sea of water baptism, became sanctified and separated from the world, and then journeyed on to receive Christ's redemptive work of divine healing. Thus, the second great giant step had been taken by the Church in the restorational walk to its "Canaan" of full maturity in Christ Jesus.

The Classical Pentecostal Movement. The movement's **purpose** was to restore the Holy Spirit to His powerful performance in the Church. By gifting the individual believer with "other tongues" in the baptism of the Holy Spirit and by releasing the gifts of the Spirit to the Church, Jesus restored the third doctrine of Christ to the Church—**the doctrine of baptisms**. The **place** of its birth was the United States, after which it spread to the world with its greatest percentage of growth among Christians in Latin America.

The Pentecostal Movement claims no single person as its founder. However, Charles F. Parham and W. H. Seymour come as close as any of the **men** involved to qualifying for the role. The **people** who participated and the **ministers** who propagated the Pentecostal truth came from the Holiness Movement churches.

The **message** was the baptism of the Holy Spirit evidenced by speaking in "other tongues." The **ministry** was the preaching of the Word accompanied by healings, miracles, speaking in other tongues and gifts of the Holy Spirit. All types of musical instruments and singing were used to promote the gospel and to worship God. The term "dancing in the spirit" became an accepted form of Spirit-directed, uncontrollable expression of praise. The new **products** used to spread this restorational truth to the ends of the earth were the automobile and the radio.

Thus, the Church advanced in its restorational journey through the wilderness to its "water from the Rock" experience. The **result** was more powerful performance in ministry, greater evangelism and the "rivers of living water" flowing out of the saints' innermost being in **other tongues**. The Pentecostal Movement was another progressive step in the walk of the eternal Church to Her promised Canaan Land.

The Latter Rain/Charismatic Movement. God's **purpose** for the Latter Rain Movement was to restore the experiential reality of the biblical practice of **laying on of hands**, thereby restoring to the Church the fourth doctrine of Christ. The **place** of its birth was Canada. It then spread throughout the United States and around the world.

Latter Rain Leaders. The Latter Rain Movement has never recognized any man or group as head of the movement, but certain **men** were notable in making known and maintaining the doctrine of laying on of hands: the laying on of hands for healing, Oral Roberts; the laying on of hands with personal prophecy by the presbytery (called a "prophetic presbytery"), Reginald Layzell; the laying on of hands with prophesying healings and miracles, William Branham.

Charismatic Leaders. Key men who were originally instrumental in activating and spreading the Charismatic renewal were Dennis Bennett, David du Plessis and Demos Shakarian. Making the historic Charismatics conscious of the reality of the spirit world of demon activity was Derek Prince. Kenneth Hagin became known as the father of the faith message for prosperity and healing.

The majority of the **people** who participated and the **ministers** who propagated deliverance evangelism and Latter Rain truths came from the Pentecostal Movement churches. Those who originally were called Charismatics were ministers and members of historic Protestant denominations, but then came those from the Catholic and Orthodox, Holiness, Evangelical and Fundamentalist churches. Finally, many Pentecostal and Latter Rain leaders reluctantly accepted the word "Charismatic" to identify those who were Holy Spirit-filled, tongues-talking, God-praising, present-truth Christians.

The Message of the Charismatic Movement. The **message** of the Charismatic renewal was threefold:
(1) The **laying on of hands** for healing, Holy Spirit baptism, deliverance, Body of Christ membership ministry and activation of the gifts of the Holy Spirit.
(2) The proclamation of all the Pentecostal and Latter Rain Movement truths to **denominational Christians.** This was mainly done by denominational ministers who were newly baptized in the Holy Spirit.
(3) The proclamation by present-truth and faith ministers of the **maturing of the Body of Christ** and of Christians **living victoriously**—spiritually, physically and financially.

The **ministry** was the preaching of the Word accompanied by healings, prophecy and revelation gifts. This caused many souls to be saved, extensive spiritual growth in individual Christians, the numerical growth of churches and the prosperity of the saints.

Time to Move On. The **result** was that the eternal Church reached its Mount Sinai experience and remained there until divine order was established so that all Christendom had an opportunity to move to the front line of present truth. The Church was encamped at that mountain of truth (Charismatic Movement) for forty years (1948-1988). The angel of the

Church in heaven has sounded the trumpet and the company of prophets are now sounding forth a clear prophetic word: "Church we have been here long enough!" (Deut.2:3).

The "Joshua Generation" is leading forth, and the priestly pastors are carrying the ark of God's restorational presence across Jordan. The journey of the Charismatic Movement has fulfilled its purpose of bringing the Church to its Jordan River. Now the cloud by day and the fire by night have been taken away, and the prophets and prophetic ministers have arisen to provide protection, direction and timing for the Church's moving. The manna has ceased, and now it is time to eat the corn of Canaan, drink the milk and be energized by the honey.

The prophetic voice is sounding forth the trumpet call: "Prepare for war; beat your pruning hooks into spears and your plowshares into swords. We have now entered into a warfare that cannot be ended until the Church of Jesus Christ has possessed the promised possessions that God has preordained for the perfected Church" (see Joel 3:9,10).

A Gigantic Final Tidal Wave of Restoration is Coming. Four major waves of restoration have taken place during the last five hundred years, with smaller waves of restoration and renewal between each of those. Several of these smaller waves of restoration and spiritual renewal of various truths and ministries have taken place since 1948—and more are coming.

A Time Unlike Any Before. The prophets, however, are seeing on the horizon of God's purpose for His Church a restorational wave of such incomprehensibly gigantic proportions—like a thousand-foot tidal wave—that it staggers the imagination and faith of both those who have prophetically seen it and those who have heard of it. It will be greater than all previous restoration movements combined. As the prophet Joel declared, there has never been a time like it before, and there never will be again (Joel 2:2).

It will be the time of Revelation 10:7: "But in the days of the voice of the seventh angel, when he shall begin to sound, the mystery of God should be finished, as he hath declared to his servants, the prophets." It will bring about the activation of Revelation 11:15: "And the seventh angel sounded; and there were great voices in heaven, saying, The kingdoms of this world are become the kingdom of our Lord, and of his Christ, and he shall reign forever and ever." It will fulfill Acts 3:19-25 concerning the restoration of all things which God has spoken by the mouth of all His holy prophets since the world began.

This time will thus fulfill all things necessary for the release of Jesus from heaven. The tidal wave of restoration headed by Christ Jesus will have such a force and height that it will sweep all evil principalities and powers from the heavenlies and wash away the kingdoms of this world. It will cause the kingdom of our Lord Jesus and His Christ-anointed Church to be established in the heavenlies and over all the earth.

The "Snowball" Principle of Restoration. If you make a hard snowball and roll it down the steep, smooth slope of a snow-covered mountainside, it begins to get bigger and go faster. That is the same way Church restoration works. The Protestant Movement was the making of the snowball at the top of the mountain. Then, with each restoration movement, the snowballing Church has become greater and the movements are happening faster. For instance, there were a thousand years of Dark Ages, then Church Restoration began in 1500. Three hundred years later, in 1800, the Holiness Movement came. Then a hundred years later, in 1900, the Pentecostal Movement appeared. Fifty years later the Latter Rain/Charismatic Movement was born. And now, since 1950, there has been a new restorational move or spiritual renewal every decade (1000-300-100-50-10).

Fivefold Ministries Restored. In each of the last five decades of the twentieth-century Church, one of the fivefold ministries (Eph.4:11) has been re-emphasized or restored, and certain biblical truths and ways of worship have been reactivated into the Church by the Holy Spirit.

DECADE	FIVEFOLD MINISTRY	MOVEMENT/REVIVAL
1950's	Evangelist	Deliverance Evangelism
1960's	Pastor	Charismatic Renewal
1970's	Teacher	Faith Teaching Movement
1980's	Prophet	Prophetic Movement
1990's	Apostle	Apostolic Movement

Even within the last forty years since the last major restoration movement, there have been men and minor movements that have added sinew to the framework of the Body of Christ. We must always keep in mind that God raises up **men** and **movements** to magnify Christ's **message** and **ministry** to His Church, not to exalt the man and the movement. But God does choose **key men** to pioneer, establish and propagate certain **truths** and **ministries** within His Church.

The Need to Restore the Fivefold Ministries. Why did the fivefold ministries need to be restored? In the past, dispensational theologians took a scripture Paul wrote to the Ephesians about apostles and prophets, and interpreted it in a way that neither Paul nor the Holy Spirit ever intended. Paul told the Ephesians that they had been brought into the Church and were built upon the founding ministry of the apostle and prophet, with Jesus Christ himself being the Chief Corner Stone from which the whole building of the Church is aligned (Eph.2:20,21).

This meant that Paul the apostle and Silas the prophet were the ones who first went to Ephesus and led them to Christ, staying there until they were established and built into a church. They exalted Christ Jesus as the sovereign head of the Church, and its Chief Corner Stone (1Pet.2:6).

Some theologians, however, improperly interpreted this scripture to say that the Church and its whole age of activity were built upon the ministry of the apostles and prophets, so that as soon as the Church, as a whole, was established (sometime within the first century), then the ministry of the apostle and prophet was finished. Therefore, those ministries were dispensationally depleted.

In this view, the Bible then became the foundation of the Church as the complete revealed will of God, thereby eliminating the founding and revealing ministry of the apostle and prophet. This position is difficult to maintain, however, because the Bible was not canonized and brought together as one book until the third century.

It was not until the restorational Latter Rain movement in 1948 that revelation and teaching was given concerning apostles and prophets. And even though those restoration brethren taught that there are prophets and apostles today, they never were willing to give public acknowledgment to those who had the gifted ministry of apostle or prophet.

Description of the Last Four Decades. I believe it is the mind of God to re-emphasize those three offices which have been accepted and somewhat understood (evangelist, pastor, teacher) and then fully clarify, amplify and magnify those two which have not been understood, accepted and recognized.

The Evangelist. In the 1950's the gifted ministry of the hour was that of the evangelist. Evangelists such as Oral Roberts were holding great tent meetings. A dual ministry of evangelism and deliverance from disease and demons provided the focus for the evangelist. Laying on of hands for healing and mass evangelism was the most prominent ministry.

During this decade the ministry of the evangelist was re-emphasized and magnified. However, within a decade the hundreds of evangelists and their large tent meetings had subsided. The great wave of restoration and amplification of the true evangelist with gifts of healing and miracles reached the shoreline of fulfillment in the 50's and receded into the ocean of the last days Church ministry.

The Pastor. The 1960's were the decade for the ministry of the pastor to be emphasized and brought to proper perspective.

Two restorational moves of the Holy Spirit contributed toward bringing this into reality. The first came in 1948 with the restorational teaching that emphasized proper divine order for the local church. Understanding came that the local church is to be self-governing and indigenous, with Christ being the sovereign head and the local pastor serving under the direct headship of Christ.

Churches also came to realize that the pastor is appointed by God and not elected by a board of elders, or deacons or by a congregation. The pastor stands in Christ's stead, and his position is not determined by the vote of those to whom he ministers, no more than the angels and twenty-four elders in heaven vote every millennium to determine whether God remains head of the universe for the next millennium. The pastor must have the freedom and authority to fulfill the vision God has given for building the local church.

The second wave that contributed to the magnification of the pastoral ministry was the Charismatic renewal that shook the whole denominational part of Christendom. Millions of denominational people were baptized with the Holy Spirit, and thousands came out of their denominations in order to walk in the fullness of present truth. In the 60's and 70's, churches would be started by Charismatic, restoration and faith ministers and within three or four years would grow to a congregation of thousands. Thus pastors became the prominent ministry of the 60's. In this way the ministry of the pastor was restored to its rightful place and magnified by the Holy Spirit to its due honor and authority.

The Teacher. The 70's were the decade for proper recognition, acceptance and magnifying of Christ's gift ministry of the teacher. The Catholic and Historic Protestant Charismatic ministers who moved into present truth were not strong evangelistic expounders in preaching like the Holiness and Pentecostal brethren. They did more teaching than preaching. So the leading ministers in the Charismatic and Faith Movements presented their truths more by teaching than by preaching.

Thousands would drive hundreds of miles to come and sit by the hour listening to one teacher after the other. Cassette tapes were made and distributed in endless numbers. The office of the **teacher** was restored to its rightful place of respect and authority, and was properly positioned as a Christ-given ministry to the Body of Christ.

The Prophet. Prophet Glenn Foster has noted that a powerful prophetic minister came through his church in the 1950's, and prophesied that the day would come when the prophets would arise and prophetic ministry would come into prominence. The prophecy also said that the prophetic movement was still thirty years away.

> One of the rare occasions when a little encouragement was offered was in the early 1950's. A certain person who had an anointed ministry came and spoke to us of a coming day of glory and power and called it, "the day of the prophets." This person said that "day" was thirty or more years down the road, for the Lord was preparing, even then, for greater things. The promise was that many mature prophetic ministries would spearhead a new day of restoration and revival. (Glenn Foster, **The Purpose and Use of Prophecy**, Glendale, Arizona, Sweetwater Publications, 1988, p. 16.)

Many of us who had been in prophetic ministry for many years had heard the same thing from God, and we looked forward to the 80's as the decade of the prophet. We were not disappointed. In the 80's the Holy Spirit began to restore Christ's ascension gifted ministry of the prophet to its proper recognition, acceptance and authority in the Church.

The prophets will be the ones to reveal the last restorational truth that shall bring the Church to maturity and finalize the preparation of the Church-Bride for the return of her Bridegroom, Jesus. The vocal and revelation gifts of the Holy Spirit were magnified by the office of the prophet in the 80's. Thus the prophets will be a corporate body fulfilling the prophecy of Malachi 4 for Christ's second coming, just as John the Baptist was the single prophet preparing the way for the Lord's first coming. The prophets will also bring revelation, restoration and preparation for the full magnification of the God-ordained office of the apostle.

The Apostle. The 1990's will be the decade for the apostle. The full restoration of the apostle in the 90's will bring a restoration of full apostolic authority and the signs and wonders of the gift of faith and the working of miracles. The Christ-ordained office and ministry of the apostle will be recognized, accepted and magnified mightily throughout the Christian world.

The discipleship/shepherding movement saw a glimpse of this truth in the 70's and tried to restore it. But many abuses occurred due to lack of balance and maturity. Nevertheless, the time for the apostle's full authority and function in the fivefold ministry will begin to come forth in the 1990's, and the end result will be unity in the Church. The reverential fear of God and His righteousness will be re-established in the Church as judgment begins at the house of God. Human-made religious kingdoms and the Babylonian system as recorded in the Bible will be shaken as God's judgments are executed by the last-day prophetic and apostolic ministries (1Pet.4:7; Acts 5:1-13; Rev. 11:3-10).

Pioneering Ministers. The last half of the twentieth century has thus far been an exciting time of restoration in the Church. Probably no other forty-year period in history has activated so many new biblical truths and ministries back into the Church. It is amazing how many of the pioneering men that span this time are still alive and active in their ministries. Here are those that represent different aspects of Holy Spirit restoration and renewal in the Church.

MEN ALIVE IN 1990 REPRESENTING FORTY YEARS OF RENEWAL

Oral Roberts	Laying on of hands for healing; seed faith
Billy Graham	Evangelism and the born-again experience
Paul Cain	Demonstration of prophets in the Church
Dick Iverson	Prophetic presbytery and the local church
T.L. Osborne	Mass evangelism with miracles
David Wilkerson	Gang and street ministry; the Jesus Movement
Demos Shakarian	Charismatic renewal among businessmen
Pat Robertson	Christian television networks; his own CBN
Paul Crouch	TBN church ministries and television evangelism
Dennis Bennett	Charismatic renewal; gift of the Holy Spirit
Charles Simpson	Discipleship, accountability and relationship
Kenneth Hagin	Faith, financial prosperity and deliverance
Yongghi Cho	Mega-churches, cell groups, intercessory prayer
Earl Paulk	Kingdom of God message, witness and ministry
Larry Lea	Daily early morning and warfare prayer
Bill Hamon	Prophets, prophetic ministry, warfare praise

With this overview of Church restoration history, we can now focus on the nature and role of the **Prophetic Movement**.

RESTORATION AND DESTINATION OF THE CHURCH

(Restoration Movements and N.T. Restorational Truths Correlated with O.T. Historical Happenings and Types)

CHURCH RESTORATION MOVEMENTS	BIBLICAL SPIRITUAL EXPERIENCES	DOCTRINES OF CHRIST (HE.6:1,2)	JOURNEYS OF THE CHILDREN OF ISRAEL	EZEKIEL'S BONE YARD (EZE.37)	WATER FROM TEMPLE (EZE.47)	TABERNACLE OF MOSES (EX.25-50)
1. Protestant	1. Justification	1. Repentance from Dead Works	1. Passover	1. Breath Enter	1. To Ankles	1. Brazen Altar
2. Holiness	2. Sanctification	2. Faith toward God	2. Red Sea, Banks, Marah-Water	2. Lay Sinew Upon You	2. To Knees	2. Laver, Table of Shewbread
3. Pentecostal	3. Manifestation	3. Doctrine of Baptisms	3. Water from Rock	3. Bring up Flesh Upon You	3. To Loins	3. Candlestick
4. Charismatic	4. Ministration	4. Laying on of Hands	4. Mt. Sinai	4. Cover You With Skin	4. To Swim In	4. Boards, Altar of Incense
CHURCH'S POSITION IN ITS RESTORATIONAL JOURNEY –		PROPHETS PREPARING THE WAY "JOSHUA GENERATION"			– FOR THE BODY OF CHRIST TO CROSS ITS JORDAN	
5. Body of Christ	5. Glorification	5. Resurrection of The Dead	5. Crossing Jordan	5. Ye Shall Live	5. Life	5. Vail and Coverings
6. Army of Lord	6. Adjudication	6. Eternal Judgment	6. Conquering Canaan	6. Exceeding Great Army	6. Miry Place Judged	6. Ark and Contents
7. Queen Church	7. Administration	7. Ultimate Perfection	7. Canaan Conquered	7. Davidic King One Shepherd	7. Rest and Life	7. Mercy Seat
8. Eternal Church	8. Continuation	8. New Earth and New Heavens	8. Ruling and Occupying Canaan	8. Tabernacle of God With Man	8. Temple of God With Man	8. New Temple

c Bishop Bill Hamon, Rt. 2, Box 351, Point Washington, FL 32454   Christian International Publishers   (FROM PAGE 309, *THE ETERNAL CHURCH*)

RESTORATION OF THE CHURCH

APPROX DATE	SPIRITUAL EXPERIENCES	DOCTRINES OF CHRIST (He.6:12; Ac.3:21)	BAPTISMS WITNESSES	RESTORATION MOVEMENTS
				AD 1500 - AD 2000+
AD 1500	**Justification** Study of Word Prayer Peace	**1 ↑ Repentance From Dead Works** Grace and Faith Eph.2:8,9	Blood	**Protestant** Lutheran Episcopal Presbyterian
AD 1800	**Sanctification** Conviction Faith, Hymns Joy, Singing	**2 ↑ Faith Toward God** Divine Faith Healing Ja.5:14,15	Water	**Holiness** Baptist Methodist (All Evangelicals) Church of God C & M Alliance
AD 1900	**Manifestation** Other Tongues Hands clapping Shouting, Fasting Dancing in Spirit Musical Instruments	**3 ↑ Doctrine of Baptism** Gifts: 1Cor.12:7-11 Message in Tongues Interpretation of Tongues	Spirit	**Pentecostal** Assembly of God Pent. Holiness Foursquare Pent. Ch. of God United Pent. Ch.
AD 1950	**Ministration** Singing-Praises Spiritual Songs Worship, Psalms Body Ministry Praise in Dance Acts of Faith Arts - Drama	**4 ↑ Laying On of Hands** Gifts: Prophecy, Healings, Faith Word of Knowledge, Word of Wisdom Laying on of Hands for: Healing Deliverance, Holy Ghost Revealing Place in Body of Christ Impartation of Gifts by Holy Spirit	Body of Christ	**Charismatic** Latter Rain Discipleship Faith Kingdom

- THE COMPANY OF PROPHETS   ...PREPARE THE WAY...   PROPHETIC MOVEMENT -

- THE COMPANY OF PROPHETS   ...PREPARE THE WAY...   PROPHETIC MOVEMENT -

DESTINATION OF THE CHURCH

APPROX DATE	SPIRITUAL EXPERIENCES	DOCTRINES OF CHRIST (He.6:1,2; Ac.3:21)	BAPTISMS WITNESSES	RESTORATION MOVEMENTS
AD 199? - Endless Ages				**AD 2000 - Eternity**
AD 199?+	**Glorification** High Praises Righteousness Agape Love Divine Unity	**5 ↑ Resurrection of the Dead** Gifts: Working of Miracles Discerning of Spirits Prelude: Purified, Spotless Full Maturity in Christ Jesus Result: Redemption of the Body Mortality Ended in Life Victory Over the Last Enemy	Fire	**Body of Christ** One United and Perfected Church
AD 20??	**Adjudication** 7-Fold Spirit	**6 ↑ Eternal Judgment** Gifts: All Gifts and Fruits Joel's Army of the Lord Manifestation of Sons of God Saints Execute Judgment Written	Love	**Army of Lord** Overcomers Bride of Christ
AD 20??	**Administration**	**7 ↑ Ultimate Perfection** God's Seventh Day of Rest 1000-year Reign of Peace on Earth Overcomers Reign With Christ	Wisdom	**Queen Church** Kingdom on Earth
ENDLESS AGES	**Continuation**	**8 ↑ New Heavens and New Earth** Redemption of Creation Restoration of the Earth Church Begins Eternal Ministry	Fullness	**Eternal Church** Universal Reign

c Bishop Bill Hamon, Rt. 2, Box 351, Point Washington, FL 32454   Christian International Publishers   (FROM PAGE 158 & 310, *THE ETERNAL CHURCH*)

5

CHARISMATIC MOVEMENT COMPARED
TO THE PROPHETIC MOVEMENT

Each restoration movement over the last five hundred years has been typified by the various experiences of the children of Israel in their journey from Egypt to their promised Canaan land (1Cor.10:1-11). The Protestant Movement parallels the Passover (salvation); the Holiness Movement, the Red Sea (water baptism), the banks (sanctification) and the waters of Marah (divine healing); the Pentecostal Movement, water from the rock (baptism of Holy Spirit); the Latter Rain Movement, Mount Sinai (prophetic presbytery). The Charismatic Movement brought everybody to Kadesh Barnea at the edge of the promised land.

The Prophetic Movement is the new Joshua Generation crossing over Jordan to go in and start possessing our prophetic-ally promised possessions. Israel was in the wilderness for thirty-eight more years after their two-year journey to reach the edge of Canaan. Because the majority did not have the faith to go in to drive out the "ites" of Canaan and possess what God had prophetically promised, they had to wander in the wilderness until a new generation could be raised up to go in (Num. 13:17-14:45).

An End Time Davidic Company. In David's time, Saul and his army had been challenged for forty days by Goliath to send him an Israelite to fight with him (1Sam.17:16). David came on the scene and went out against him with faith in God, a proven ministry, and the prophetic word of judgment which brought about Goliath's downfall. David was a prophet (Acts 2:30) and went against the enemy not in his own strength, but in the name of the Lord. He depended on God to defend His own cause through enabling him to defeat the giant who was defying God's people.

Today God is raising up a Davidic company of believers who will not be afraid to step out from among the crowd of religious people like Saul's army and become instruments in God's hand to destroy the giant worldly satanic system that is defying God's purpose for His people. The Joshua generation with a Davidic dedication and faith are now crossing over Jordan to face the giants living in their promised land of Canaan. The Prophetic Movement does not only have the new generation, but also older, mature ministers with the Joshua and Caleb spirit who believe that "we are well able" to do all that God prophetically promised we could. They are the mature prophetic and apostolic leaders whom God is bringing to the forefront to lead the younger generation into the conquest of Canaan.

The Charismatic and Prophetic Movements Compared. The Charismatic Movement was the time when God was giving Christians in all denominations an opportunity to be established in all present truth and to receive all spiritual experiences that have been restored to the Church during the last five hundred years. It was the time when the Church was "circling around" until everyone had an opportunity to be updated, and a new generation prepared. The Prophetic Movement, on the other hand, is the company of prophets leading the Church across Jordan to start possessing their promised Canaan. The Charismatic Movement produced a multitude of independent ministries and churches. In the Prophetic Movement we are seeing a new recognition of the need for networking together in a 'unity of faith' (Eph.4:13) and allowing 'fathers' in the faith to arise and give leadership, oversight and covering (1Cor.4:15). As Malachi prophesied: the spirit of Elijah "will turn the heart of the fathers to the children, and the heart of the children to the their fathers, lest I come and smite the earth with a curse."

(Mal.4:6) As the angel declared in Luke, this will help " to make ready a people prepared for the Lord" (Lk.1:17). With this in mind, we can make the following comparison.

Wilderness Walkers vs. Canaan Conquerors. In the wilderness the manna fell from heaven; all the people had to do was gather it and eat. In Canaan, corn had to be parched, cows milked and beehives robbed in order to enjoy the land flowing with milk and honey. The Charismatic Movement walked in the revelation of praising God for His presence. But the Prophetic Movement has moved into the revelation of warfare praise for pulling down strongholds of the enemy. We have discovered that pro-phetic praise to God is His jamming device to confuse the communication channels of the enemy so that they get confused and kill one another as the enemy armies did when Jehoshaphat's people went against them with warfare praise (2Chr.20:12-25).

In the wilderness the people had miracles for preservation, while in Canaan they had miracles for possessing. In the wilder-ness the primary process was updating and maintaining, but in Canaan it was advancing and taking the kingdom by the force of faith. Before the people were wandering wilderness-walkers, but now the challenge is for us to be courageous Canaan-conquerors.

Apostolic Cloud and Prophetic Fire. In the wilderness journey the people were covered and protected by a cloud by day and warmed, enlightened and directed by a fire by night. But for the Prophetic Movement in Canaan, the Apostle is the covering and protecting cloud and the Prophet is the enlightening and direct-ing fire. That is one reason why apostles and prophets must be restored before the Church can fulfill its predestinated end-time purpose on earth.

Warfare Intensified. In the wilderness the people had constant refreshing with occasional battles. But in Canaan it is constant warfare with occasional times of refreshing. In the past it was freedom to do your own thing, but now it is faithfulness to fight as a soldier without breaking rank (Joel 2:7). In the wilderness it was rejoicing in our freedom from religious slavery, but now it is repenting of our selfishness, laying down our rights and allowing His righteousness to be worked in us.

The **company of prophets** is called to be like the U.S. Marines who go before the main army to secure a beachhead for a landing. They are called with the commission from Christ to be the prophetic David company who put their lives on the line to destroy the opposing giant so that the rest of God's army will arise and drive the enemy out of their land. They are like Jonathan and his armor bearer and Gideon's three hundred: They exposed themselves to the enemy, then they saw God move in miraculous ways so that the enemy began to flee. Then the other Israelites could join them to destroy the enemy completely.

Prophets and warfare praisers are called to go out before the regular army. They must not only overcome by the blood of the Lamb and the word of their testimony, but they must also have come to stage number three, **where they love not their lives unto the death** (Rev.12:11; 17:14).

Prophets are like pioneers and space explorers: They "boldly go where no man has ever gone before." That is one reason why they suffer more persecution and are more often misunderstood than other ministers. Perhaps that is the reason why James said for us to "take, my brethren, the prophets who have spoken in the name of the Lord, for an example of suffering affliction and of patience" (Ja.5:10).

None of us in our natural mind would want to be a prophet; we would have to be in the mind of Christ instead. The faint-hearted and fearful should not attach themselves to the prophets or the Prophetic Movement, for they have now entered a warfare that will not cease until all the "ites" of Canaan have been removed and the kingdoms of this world have become the kingdoms of our Lord Jesus Christ and His victorious Church (Deut.20:8; Jdg.7:3; Rev.11:15).

6

WHAT IS THE PROPHETIC MOVEMENT
ALL ABOUT?

The Prophetic Movement is part of the Holy Spirit's continuing work of bringing the Church to full restoration. The restoration of Christ's ascension gift of **prophet** is absolutely essential for God's full purpose in the Church to be accomplished. It is not just the restoration of a fivefold ministry, but the bringing forth of a whole company of those prophetic ministers. The prophets will inspire all fivefold ministers to be more prophetic in their ministries.

The Role of Prophets in Restoration. The company of prophets will help restore the apostles back into their rightful place in the Church. The full restoration of apostles and prophets back into the Church will then bring divine order, unity, purity and maturity to the corporate Body of Christ. The saints will be equipped and activated in the supernatural power of God to be a witness and demonstration to all nations of the powerful kingdom of God.

That will in turn bring about the end of this world system of humanity and Satan's rule. The fulfillment of all these things will release Christ, who has been seated at the right hand of the Father in heaven, to return literally and set up His everlasting kingdom over all the earth. As the prophet Daniel foretold, the stone (the Church) that was hewn out of the mountain (Christ) will continue to grow in strength and momentum like the snowball rolling down the mountain, until it hits the feet of the giant world empires—causing them to crumble and come into submission to Christ Jesus (Dan.2:44).

What Does the Prophetic Movement Include? The Prophetic Movement includes all realms of the prophetic: prophets, prophetic ministers, prophetic people, personal prophecy, the prophetic presbytery, gifts of the Holy Spirit, prophetic worship, prophetic song, as well as expressive praise signing and dancing, pageantry and numerous ways of worshiping God in the arts and drama. Thus the movement touches on all natural and supernatural means of communicating God's word, will and miraculous ministry to humankind. It also involves the continuing work of purifying and perfecting the saints (that is, all believers) in Christ's character, as well as the activation of Church members and ministers into their highest calling in Christ Jesus.

The Prophetic Movement is to proclaim God's prophets, propagate the prophetic, activate others to become prophetic ministers and produce a prophetic people for God's purpose. All of these restored Prophetic Movement truths and ministries are built upon and operate from all the fundamental biblical doctrines, truths and ministries that have been restored within the Church during the last five hundred years.

Covet the Prophetic Ministry. The Apostle Paul uses the word "prophesy" to be representative of the whole prophetic ministry. It is the only ministry that Christians are scripturally commanded to covet: **"Covet to prophesy"** (1Cor.14:39).

Other scriptures tell us not to "be ignorant of the prophetic ministry but to have an experiential working knowledge of it" (1Cor.12:1); to "earnestly desire" it (1Cor.12:31); and to be "zealous" for prophetic ministry (1Cor.14:12). We are to make divine "agape" love, which is Christ-like character, our progressive ultimate goal while continually desiring and ministering spiritual gifts, especially prophesying—which is the key gift that opens the door to prophetic ministry (1Cor.14:1).

Despise Not, Quench Not. Ministers and all Christians are commanded to take a believing and appreciating attitude toward prophesying, for God says "despise **not** prophesying" and "quench **not** the Spirit" (1Thess.5:19,20). When prophetic ministry is despised it quenches (restricts, subdues, suppresses, hinders) the Holy Spirit from fulfilling His prophetic commission from Christ Jesus. Prophet Joel prophesied that in the last days God would pour out His Spirit upon all flesh, and our sons and daughters would prophesy (Joel 2:28,29). The Apostle Peter, by divine inspiration, declared that "those days" were that of the Church Age (Acts 2:17; He.1:2).

Numerous Scriptures About Prophecy. There are more New Testament scriptures that talk about the prophetic ministry and instructions concerning it than there are about some of the other vital biblical truths that Christians practice regularly, such as communion, water baptism, church membership, tithes and offerings and music ministry. Meanwhile, churches do a number of things that cannot be based on a single example in the New Testament, such as church music specials, Sunday schools, worship with musical instruments, Charismatic "praise dance" or Pentecostal "dancing in the Spirit," choirs, a written order for a complete church service, Christian weddings—even Christian funerals (at the only three funerals we are told Jesus attended, He raised the dead back to life; is that our example?). In addition we could mention all the things churches do today with our modern electronics, modes of travel and mass media.

Acceptable and Practical Though No Scriptural Example. These are all acceptable practices in most churches today, though there are no examples and very few scriptures relating to these activities in the New Testament. But there are numerous scriptures and examples in the New Testament concerning the prophetic ministry. So why shouldn't all Christians who base their faith and practice upon the Bible accept this New Testament prophetic ministry and practice it as easily as they do the Lord's Supper, water baptism, or paying tithes?

Prophetic Ministers. Present-truth **prophetic ministers** are those ministers who are not called to the office of prophet but nevertheless believe there are apostles and prophets in the Church today, and they move in the supernatural gifts of the Holy Spirit. They can minister prophetically by the gift of prophecy and word of knowledge, or any of the other gifts which the Holy Spirit has willed to them as part of their spiritual heritage. All fivefold ministers are called and enabled to minister prophetically by prophetic preaching, revelation knowledge, gifts of the Spirit, and their ascension gift enablement.

Prophetic Saints and Prophetic People. You do not have to be one of Christ's ascension gifts of apostle, prophet, evangelist, pastor or teacher to be a **prophetic saint**. Prophetic saints have one or more of the Holy Spirit gifts, ministries and other divine enablements for service in God's kingdom. **Prophetic people** are those saints who have been educated, motivated and activated into their membership ministries in the Body of Christ.

Covet to Prophesy. When the Apostle Paul tells the saints in the Corinthian church to **covet to prophesy**, he has more in mind than some Pentecostal concepts of prophetic ministry. The understanding among most Pentecostal denominations in the past has been strictly the use of the vocal gifts of tongues, interpretation of tongues and prophecy in ministering to the congregation. In the Pentecostal Movement churches they mainly had tongues and interpretation in a service. They taught that a message in tongues with the interpretation was the same as prophesying, that is, God expressing His thoughts to the people present.

In Latter Rain churches they had hardly any tongues and interpretation, but they had frequent prophesying during each church service. Charismatic and Faith churches had a combination of both. The old concept is to stand up in the congregation and speak out loud a prophetic word of exhortation, edification and comfort. These congregational prophecies are usually given during or at the end of the worship part of the church service.

New Ways to Minister Prophetically. These practices are biblical and valid, but they are only one application and dimension of the prophetic ministry. Prophesying is expressing God's heart, thoughts, desires, intents and specific words at the proper time in the right place to the person or people God has ordained to receive His message. God is now revealing and adding many new ways and means of ministering prophetically.

In chapter five of volume one in this series, *Prophets and Personal Prophecy*, five biblical sources or instruments of prophetic ministry are described: (1) The office and ascension gift of **prophet**; (2) **prophetic preaching**; (3) the **prophetic presbytery**; (4) the Holy Spirit **gift of prophecy**; and (5) the **spirit of prophecy and prophetic song**. Only the prophet can minister in the authority, office and dimension of prophet, but all other ministers can function in the other realms.

Developing Saints in their Gifts. The **prophetic movement** also brought with it the revelation and application for activating saints in their gifts of the Holy Spirit. One of the characteristics of a true restorational movement (see chapter 7 for the others) is that the Holy Spirit gives the divine wisdom and ability to the leaders to develop others in the spiritual gift or ministry being restored.

The **Protestant Movement** brought the **gift of eternal life** from the few to the many. It also brought the biblical knowledge of how to lead others into the gift of eternal life. Later movements revealed more ways of drawing upon the quality of that gift of life for victorious living.

The **Pentecostal Movement** did the same for the **gift of the Holy Spirit** with the consequent manifestation of speaking in other tongues. Pentecostals brought it from the obscure few to the many by the revelation knowledge that it was for all that had received the gift of eternal life. But it was not until the Charismatic Renewal that revelation knowledge and application came for taking it into every Christian denomination—even to the pre-restoration Catholics.

Charismatics also received more faith principles for administering the gift of the Holy Spirit to others. A restoration truth takes a gift out of the sole sovereignty of God and releases divine principles to spiritual men and women of God concerning how to receive and minister that gift to others. This is not a matter of submitting God's sovereignty to human faith, nor of limiting saints to operate in spiritual gifts only when the Holy Spirit sovereignly wills, but simply moving in the gifts given by divine faith and grace (Rom.12:6; Eph.2:8,9).

Training in Operation of the Gifts. Classical Pentecostals and Charismatics believe they can biblically educate someone about the Holy Spirit baptism and then help pray that person through to speaking in tongues. They will even give them step-by-step instructions and acts of faith to take to activate the Holy Spirit gift of their own prayer and praise language.

In a similar way, the **Prophetic Movement** is bringing the revelation knowledge, methods, ways and means of teaching, activating and maturing saints in their **gifts of the Holy Spirit** and spiritual ministries. I have conducted hundreds of special schools of the Holy Spirit for this purpose and have numerous testimonies from church members and ministers that it works. The following chart summarizes these three gifts and the movement that restored each to this level.

GIFT	DATE	MOVEMENT
Gift of Eternal Life	1500	Protestant Movement
Gift of the Holy Spirit	1900	Pentecostal Movement
Gifts of the Holy Spirit	1990	Prophetic Movement

Protestant Movement churches thus were established by God to provide a much-needed place where the saints could hear positive revelation teaching concerning this gift, enabling them to believe for and receive the gift of eternal life. **Pentecostal Movement churches** arose to provide revelation preaching in a place where believers could believe for and receive the gift of the Holy Spirit. And **Prophetic Movement churches** are being established by God today to provide a place for the fivefold ministries to be manifest so that they can do their job of equipping the saints. These churches are teaching, training and activating believers in the use of the gifts of the Holy Spirit.

Time to Activate the Saints. Ministers who are seeking to keep step with the Holy Spirit in His restorational work in the Church must begin activating the saints into their gifts and callings. We are called not only to purify the Church, but also to mature and equip the Church for the Day of the Lord. We are being challenged to raise up soldiers for God's army—not to prepare people for retirement and an eternal heavenly vacation as "hallelujah hoboes."

Fivefold ministers are expressly commissioned by God to perfect, mature and equip the saints (Eph.4:11,12). So we must train them in the use of the gifts of the Holy Spirit, our weapons of warfare. Sadly enough, for centuries Christian ministers have only sought to clothe the saints with their Christian armor (Eph.6:10-18). But the armor is not enough—it is mainly only for defensive purposes, to protect and preserve.

The only offensive item in the armor is the sword of the Spirit, which is the Word of God. So the vocal, revelation and power gifts of the Spirit must be activated with the other expressions of God's powerful word for us to properly do spiritual warfare. This is the time for the gifts to become an active, integral part of the life and ministry of every saint.

A Serious Matter. This is how serious I am convinced the Holy Spirit is about this matter: I believe He has said that the churches and ministers who do not work with Him to fulfill this commission from Christ will decline. If pastors refuse to equip their saints in the gifts, then either they will be removed from the pastorate, or the people who desire the gifts will be removed from their congregations and given to other pastors who will do the will of God.

All the excuses given in the past for failing to activate the saints into the gifts of the Holy Spirit will be unacceptable to

Christ. He is determined to bring all the members in His Body into their membership ministry (Acts 17:30).

Some ministers say that activation of the saints brings confusion, and that the saints are not mature enough to be allowed to minister in the gifts. But if the saints are not mature and properly prepared, then who is to blame—the people or the pastor? Saints only learn by doing; "by reason of use [they] have their senses exercised to discern both good and evil" (He.5:14).

Of course, it is easier to birth children of God than to mature them into manhood and ministry. But that is part of the work of the ministry. We ministers of this generation will be held accountable and responsible before God for restoring the gifts of the Holy Spirit to every saint.

Teaching vs. Activating. We are not just talking about teaching the saints. Present-truth believers have been taught about the gifts of the Spirit for the last eighty years. Teaching alone does not fulfill the minister's responsibility anymore. All present-truth ministers must now motivate, activate and mature the saints in their gifts and calling.

We have dressed the Bride of Christ properly in her garment of praise. Now it is time to develop her in the gifts of the Spirit to the extent that we have developed them in worship and praise. It is time to advance beyond just singing choruses about the army of the Lord to actually training saints in their weapons of warfare.

Ways and means of doing this are now being revealed. Schools and seminars and prophetic churches are activating saints in numerous places. This is the time of visitation for the full manifestation of the gifts in every minister and saint.

A PERSONAL TESTIMONY

All Believers Can Be Trained. My personal experience with prophetic ministry over the years—beginning with my Pentecostal experience and then on into the Latter Rain Movement in the fifties—illustrates well the way in which the Prophetic

Movement has come to demonstrate that all believers can be trained to practice the gifts of the Holy Spirit.

I was saved and baptized in the Holy Spirit at a brush arbor meeting in Oklahoma on my sixteenth birthday, in 1950. For the next two years I attended Pentecostal churches, where I was established in Pentecostal doctrine and ways of worship.

Latter Rain Grounding. In 1952 I began attending a church that was moving in the direction of the Latter Rain Movement, which was sweeping through Pentecostal churches of the time. Latter Rain congregations were characterized by singing of choruses, melodious praises, personal prophecy and the prophetic presbytery.

Experiencing the Prophet. My first exposure to receiving personal prophecy from a prophet was in 1952. I began to prophesy consistently in the congregation after that. In 1953 I began attending a Bible college in Portland, Oregon, that was also participating in the Latter Rain Movement. At the college were several teachers and prophets. While I was there, I received an extended personal prophecy from three faculty ministers—when transcribed, the prophecies ran for several pages—and these words prophesied my calling, gifts and ministry.

Pastoral Ministry. After I left Bible college I pastored a small church for six years in Washington State. During this time I attended the annual Crescent Beach Conferences, which taught about the function of prophetic presbyteries (1Tim.4:14) according to the understanding of the restoration and Revival Fellowship Churches. I became well-founded in the teaching and practice of these churches, which provided certain guidelines and procedures for candidates who desired to receive the laying on of hands and prophecy by prophetic presbyteries.

Prophetic Presbytery Customs. The experiential truth of personal prophecy had been sovereignly restored by God back to the Church in February 1948 (see the history of this event in

The Eternal Church, chapter 10, "The Latter Rain Movement"). In subsequent years, several patterns, customs and procedures had gradually evolved with regard to personal prophetic ministry. These were similar to those practiced at the Bible college where I had received prophetic ministry in 1953.

At the college, the president announced on a Sunday that prophetic presbytery would be provided the following Thursday evening. Anyone desiring to be a candidate for prophetic ministry had to fast a minimum of three days in order to be considered for such ministry. I fasted more days than required for candidacy. On Thursday evening we candidates entered into a time of prayer and praise that lasted about an hour.

Next, the ministers who were to form the prophetic presbytery joined in prayer, getting into a huddle like football players. They called one man out of the group, had him kneel at a chair, and prayed for a few minutes over him. Then they prophesied over him. Finally, they prayed to "seal" the prophetic words spoken over him and had him return to his seat.

The ministers went back into their prayer huddle again while the congregation prayed and praised the Lord. Then after several minutes one of the ministers called me out to be the next candidate. They followed the same procedure, except that after I received prophetic ministry they had me stand and prophesy as well.

After I returned to my seat, one of the ministers announced that they believed the two of us were the only ones God wanted to receive prophetic ministry that night. Almost a hundred students had fasted for three days with great expectations of receiving personal prophecy, and so the others were deeply discouraged; some were even resentful. To make matters worse, that was the only prophetic presbytery conducted for the entire school year.

A Holy Spirit Maximum? During the next twenty years, I helped conduct a number of prophetic presbyteries and ministered individually as a prophet to a number of people. During this time, I never prophesied over more than ten people in one setting or service. Four to six couples, or ten or twelve individuals, were the most I had ever seen ministered to during a single prophetic presbytery session. So I thought that was somehow the "divine order" for the prophetic or perhaps the Holy Spirit's maximum number for a single service. But the Lord burst my "old wineskin" in this regard when in 1973 I experienced a sovereign move of God in my life.

In October of 1972 I received a personal prophecy from a prophet who said that within three months I would receive a visitation from God that would open up an endless flow of prophecy out of me. The prophecy said it would be such a flow that it would continue from one day into the next. At times I would have to take a break, then come back at a designated time to continue prophesying over numerous people hour after hour.

A Sovereign Move of God. In January of 1973 I went from our Christian International headquarters in San Antonio, Texas, to attend the annual Revival Fellowship Conference in Yuba City, California. After the conference I stopped to visit a minister in Sacramento. There, a student I had taught in Bible college— Evangelist David Cook—was preaching the last two nights of a two-week revival. He had no idea I was coming, because I had not planned to be in Sacramento or in that particular church. God's providence had simply dropped me off there unexpectedly.

David had mentioned at the beginning of the revival that he felt God wanted to speak to many in the church through personal prophecy. But he told them he didn't know how that could happen, because he himself didn't prophesy, and the only person he knew who was a prophet and could minister to people in personal prophecy was one of his Bible college teachers in Texas. So you can imagine his surprise and excitement when he saw me enter the church building!

David had me lead the people in worship to get them liberated into praise dancing and rejoicing before the Lord. He explained to me what he had told the people and asked if I would prophesy over some of them as the Lord directed. So over the next hour and a half I called out about four couples and several individuals to receive personal prophecy.

Old Wineskin Broken. That was the most I had ever seen ministered to in one service, so I thought the Holy Spirit had reached His maximum for the night. But because most of the people present had never experienced or even seen a manifestation of personal prophecy, I suggested that they all form a circle around the meeting room as the ministers formed a double row in front. Then everyone could at least pass through the rows of ministers and have us lay hands on them to ask God's blessing on them.

As I laid hands on the first person, the spirit of prophecy began to stir and boil within my spirit. Prophetic words began to fill my mind for the person. But my "old wineskin" of past procedures and experience reminded me that I had already ministered to the maximum for one service. So I restrained myself from prophesying to that individual. But the same thing happened when I laid hands on the next two.

Quench Not the Prophetic Flow. When I laid hands on the fourth one, there was such a strong bubbling forth of the prophetic anointing and such a flow of prophetic thoughts for the person that I began to debate with God in my mind concerning what was happening. I told Him that I had not asked for this, and I asked whether it was His sovereign move. Was I supposed to release this prophetic flow to the people?

He spoke clearly and told me to allow the prophetic flow to go out to the people as long as it kept bubbling forth. So I did. That fourth person received a prophecy, and so did all the rest. The first three even got back into line to receive the prophetic ministry that the prophet hadn't had faith to give them the first time. All eighty-five people present that night received the laying on of hands with personal prophecy. It was 2:30 a.m. when the last one had received ministry.

Thus the prophecy I had received came to pass: Within three months I had flowed prophetically from one day into the next.

The Flow Continues. That night I thought this was a sovereign move of God never to be repeated again. But just two weeks later I was in Pennsylvania, where a hundred and fifty people had gathered to hear prophetic ministry. I preached for an hour and fifteen minutes, and then I felt led to pray for a few of the people. As I began to lay hands on the people, the prophetic anointing began to arise mightily within me. It continued until 3:00 a.m., when the one-hundred-and-fiftieth person received the laying on of hands and prophetic ministry.

After that service, everywhere I went God moved in a similar way. There were very few services during the next twelve years in which I was not still prophesying over people until after midnight.

Training and Activating Others. In 1984 we began conducting Christian International seminars where a prophetic presbytery was provided for all who attended. At the first few seminars I prophesied over all those attending, and the ten or twelve Christian International ministers present would stand with me and occasionally give a short prophecy or word of knowledge. But by 1987 the ministerial staff and attending prophetic ministers had matured with experience and wisdom sufficient to lead prophetic teams. By the time of the May 1989 prophetic conference, we had Christian International ministers forming twelve prophetic teams who prophesied to four hundred and fifty seminar attendees in two afternoons.

Since Christian International does not yet have sufficient motel rooms on its campus to accommodate all those attending seminars, our seminar meetings are held at local motels with large meeting rooms. These are conducted with the proper covering of the apostolic-prophet overseer of the Christian International-Network of Prophetic Ministries, the pastor of the Christian International Church, and the ministerial staff of the organization. In these seminars and other settings, we have personally trained over a hundred prophets who are flowing prophetically by the hour to numerous people, just as I did for the twelve years I traveled continuously throughout the United States and many foreign countries.

How Does It Work? Some people who have never ministered prophetically in this manner cannot understand how a time and place can be set to prophesy over people. Even some who have participated in a prophetic presbytery cannot understand how our prophets can prophesy over all those who come before them in a ministry session.

I must admit that I cannot find words to explain in detail how it works any more than I can explain in natural logic how I was born again and became a new creature in Christ Jesus. I cannot fully explain how I received the Holy Spirit prayer language simply by asking, believing and receiving from Jesus Christ. I don't know how it is that I can pray in that prayer language any time I want to.

But I **do** know that eternal life, the Holy Spirit and unknown tongues are divine gifts or enablements. And Christ's gifts simply enable the human spirit to operate within the ability of Christ.

Given, Not Lent. Peter declares that we are made partakers of Christ's own divine nature (2Pet.1:4). Paul declares that each Christian has received a special manifestation of the Holy Spirit (the nine gifts of the Holy Spirit; 1Cor.12:7-11). These are not **lent** to the saints; they are **given**. The fivefold ascension gifts of Jesus and the gifts of the Holy Spirit are manifestations of Christ's divine nature. The redeemed human spirit is invested with special enablements and characteristics of Christ's divine nature and ministering ability.

Thus the person who receives the **gift of prophecy** has his or her redeemed, baptized spirit enabled with that part of Christ's Spirit that made Him able to speak the mind of God at the right time to the right people. Those who receive the gift of healing have the ability that enabled Christ to lay hands on the sick and heal them. So if you receive revelation knowledge concerning which special enablement you have received, and you believe that you truly have that divine ability, then you can minister that ability to individuals according to the proportion of the faith you exercise. Paul says, "If a man's gift is prophesying, let him use it in proportion to his faith" (Rom.12:6).

In a similar way, the fruit of the Spirit we receive when we are born again does not automatically grow. We must have faith and yieldedness to draw upon God's love, joy, peace, patience and all the other fruit.

Everything by Faith. Every divine attribute and ability is thus received, activated and ministered by faith. "Without faith it is impossible to please God" (He.11:6). Hebrews 11 declares that all the great men and women of God of old accomplished all their great feats for God by **faith**.

Once an individual receives one of the fivefold gifted ministries of apostle, prophet, evangelist, pastor or teacher, he or she receives that part of Christ's own divine ability in that area. A **pastor** receives Christ's own good shepherd nature and ability to shepherd any time at any place to anyone of God's sheep in his flock. The **evangelist** has Christ's ability to minister eternal life to any receptive person at any time. A **prophet** has had his or her spirit enabled with the capability of Christ's prophetic Spirit or nature that made Him able to know things about people that cannot be known by natural knowledge; to discern callings and ministries that God's people have received; and to speak the future counsels and purposes of God.

Spirit of the Prophet Subject to the Prophet. Jesus was not moved to minister just by the needs of the people, rather by the leading of the Father (Jn.5:19,20). Even though everything is by grace and faith and by divine enablement, yet it is not always timely, in order or the leading of the Spirit for gifts to be manifested and prophecies to be given. The spirit of the prophet is subject to the prophet both in restraint and activation. It is incumbent upon the discernment and discretion of the prophetic minister to determine if prophetic ministry is timely, prudent or appropriate (1Cor.14:32).

God Knows Everything About Every Person. Every saint has divine gifts, talents and ministries, and God has counsels and purposes for every member in the Body of Christ. Therefore a **prophet or prophetess** can prophesy some of these things to any Christian who comes before him or her. The prophet prophesies according to his developed spiritual senses and matured faith to minister according to his or her particular gifting from God.

Can You Make God Talk? Someone once asked my wife, "How can your husband prophesy over every person he lays hands upon? Can he 'by faith' make God talk to anyone at any time?" She explained that I am not **making** God talk at my will when I prophesy any more than speaking in tongues is **making** the Holy Spirit talk every time the Spirit-baptized believer desires to pray in the Spirit.

Father God Always Has Something to Say to His Children. To illustrate how there could be a word for everyone, she suggested an earthly parallel in our relationships at home: "If you were a parent of ten children," she asked, "and each one came and stood before you wanting to hear from you, wouldn't you have something to say to each one? You might speak just a word of approval to one, and say simply, 'I love you,' to another; while to others you might take the opportunity to give several pages of instruction, correction, encouragement and direction.

"A true father would not just look at one of the children and say nothing, or declare, 'I'm sorry; I just can't think of a thing to say to you.' I believe Christ Jesus takes every opportunity He can to communicate His thoughts and intents toward His children."

The Nabi Prophet. We have much to learn about the different types of prophets—some are "seers" who prophesy according to visions, dreams or other revelation knowledge they have received; others are what I would call the "nabi" prophet, from the Hebrew word for prophet that means "to bubble forth." A nabi prophet knows in part and prophesies in part; most of the time when he or she sees with the eyes of the Spirit, it is like looking "through a glass darkly" (1Cor.13:9,12).

I am a nabi prophet; when I prophesy to numerous people one right after the other, I do not minister by visions, dreams or other knowledge previously received. Instead, I receive the words directly from my divinely enabled spirit just as I do when I speak in tongues (1Cor.14:14,15). I see the thoughts about to be expressed in words only micro-seconds before they are spoken—just enough time to decide whether I have faith to speak it, whether I am using the proper phrasing, and whether it would be wise to speak what I am perceiving (1Cor.14:32; Rom.12:6).

Personally, I rarely receive much revelation knowledge about a person before I lay hands on that person and begin to prophesy. My natural mind has no way of knowing whether or not the things being prophesied are accurate. I have envied prophets like William Branham, Kenneth Hagin and more recently, Paul Cain, who have received their prophetic information in a vivid dream or vision, or from an angel. But in their case as in mine, faith is necessary: They must have faith to repeat what they have seen or heard, while I must have faith to open my mouth moment by moment and minister out of the Holy Spirit's gifting.

I have even fasted and prayed, begging God to give me more visions, dreams and divine facts in the natural understanding. But He has continually told me that He has not called me to function as that type of prophet. Instead, He has called me to be a prophet that will function in the way that enables people to be taught, activated, trained and matured in their divinely-ordained prophetic ministry.

Teaching Others to Minister Prophetically. The way I prophesy by faith and grace has enabled me to teach other prophets and prophetic ministers how to exercise their spiritual senses (He. 5:14) to a greater perception, and to grow in grace and knowledge (2Pet.3:18) to increase their faith to manifest more of the mind of Christ to others (1Cor.2:16; 1Pet.4:11). I have taught, trained and activated hundreds of prophets into their fivefold prophet calling. I have found that those **called to be prophets** can be trained to be prophets just as those **called to be pastors, evangelists or teachers** can be trained in their God-ordained calling.

Many of these prophets even had limitations and mindsets in the beginning concerning when, where and how many people at a time they could minister to. But after I worked with them awhile, they too could stand by the hour and minister to every person on whom they were directed to lay their hands.

God's Word Stands. I must say that even though I have fussed at God sometimes for making me prophesy by faith, trusting wholly in the Holy Spirit's inspiration and Christ's prophet gift ability, He has been faithful to speak accurately with great anointing so that very few of the prophecies given seem to fall to the ground or fail to come to pass. The dilemma for the prophets is that, if they imply infallibility then they are branded as heretics, but if they demonstrate their fallibility by missing it, then they are declaimed as false prophets (1Sam.3:19; Deut. 18:20-22; see chapter 9).

Proof in the Fruit of the Ministry. I have now prophesied to approximately 20,000 individuals, yet I have had less than one tenth of one percent (approximately 20 individuals) ever accused me in person or by letter of completely missing the mark in what I prophesied to them. (I am sure the percentage would be much higher if there had been opportunity to follow up on each one ministered to.) Many of these prophecies have revealed ten to fifteen facts about a person's past, present or future. I have prophesied revelation knowledge concerning physical conditions, and there are numerous testimonies of healings and miracles, some even for incurable diseases. The report I hear most from people to whom I have prophesied is this: "The word you gave me was right on, is coming to pass and is working in my life."

You ask how I can prophesy to anyone at any time? By

God's divine gifting, grace and faith—the same way I received and function in the gift of eternal life and the gift of the Holy Spirit. Of course, I am still subject to the unction, wisdom, discretion and divine release of Christ to minister prophetically.

A Prophetic People Properly Equipped. Before the Prophetic Movement has finished its course, saints everywhere will be consistently ministering the gifts of the Holy Spirit, just as the Protestant Movement brought consistent ministering of the gift of eternal life and the Pentecostal and Charismatic Movements ministered consistently the gift of the Holy Spirit, with its prayer and praise language for personal edification.

God prophetically showed me that He really wants a prophetic people equipped in their weapons of warfare, including the gifts of the Holy Spirit. In the 1990's all true present-truth ministers will receive Christ's vision and burden for equipping the Church in the prophetic ministry of the gifts of the Holy Spirit. Times and places will be provided for teaching, activating, training and maturing saints to minister spiritual gifts in a proper and timely way.

Soldiers learn how to use their weapons of warfare at their military base in their own country before going out to fight the enemy outside their country. Saints must learn how to exercise gifts in their church meetings before they minister them out in the city streets.

The Fivefold Ministry Equips. The fivefold ministry was established and set in the Church for the equipping of the saints in their membership ministries so that the whole Body of Christ will come to maturity in manhood and ministry (Eph.4:11-13). This will fulfill one of the purposes of the Prophetic Movement: "to make ready a people" for the coming of the Lord (Lk.1:17). Christ Jesus gave apostles, prophets, evangelists, pastors and teachers for the equipping of the saints in their ministries so that the whole Body of Christ can come to maturity (Eph.4:11).

The Gospel of the Kingdom. The last message to be preached before the literal coming of Christ is the "**gospel of the kingdom** [which] must be preached in all the world for a witness, then shall the end come" (Mt.24:14). This gospel will not be preached and demonstrated by just a few great evangelist ministers or powerful prophets and apostles. The Scriptures reveal that it is mainly the **saints** who will take the kingdom message and ministry to all the world.

No longer will we focus on a few mighty ministers or a one-man show; instead, "the **saints** of the most High shall take the kingdom [message] and possess [demonstrate] the kingdom forever" (Dan.7:18) so that everyone can see Jesus demonstrated as King over all the domains of earth.

"Judgment was given to the **saints** of the most High; and the time came that the **saints** possessed the **kingdom**" (Dan.7:22). "And the kingdom and dominion, and the greatness of the kingdom under the whole heaven, shall be given to the **people** of the **saints** of the Most High, whose **kingdom** is an everlasting **kingdom**, and all dominions shall serve and obey him" (Dan. 7:27).

The end result will be the fulfillment of Daniel 2:44 and Revelation 11:15: "And in the days of these kings shall the God of heaven set up a **kingdom** which shall never be destroyed: and the **kingdom** shall not be left to other people, but it shall break in pieces and consume all these kingdoms, and it shall stand forever." "The kingdoms of this world are become the **kingdom** of our Lord, and of his Christ; and he shall reign for ever and ever" (Rev.11:15).

The Last Great Harvest Reaped by the Saints. Those prophetic **saints** will fulfill the prayer that Jesus taught them to pray and pursue: "Thy **kingdom come**, Thy will be done **on earth** as it is in **heaven**" (Mt.6:10). Jesus revealed in his parable of the Great Supper that the last worldwide revival will be that of the **saints** going out into the highways and byways, compelling the people to come in by the convincing supernatural gifts of God so that Christ's house (the Church) may be filled (Lk.14:16-23). The last great harvest will be reaped not only by fivefold ministers but by the **people** with apostolic power and prophetic ministry of the supernatural.

7

SEVEN PRINCIPLES
OF A
TRUE RESTORATION MOVEMENT

There is a difference between a new restoration movement of the Holy Spirit and a revival or renewal of truths and biblical experiences which have already been restored during the last five hundred years of Church restoration. In order for a certain activity of the Holy Spirit to be called a **Restorational Movement**, it must contain certain elements and accomplish specific things. There are at least seven major characteristics of a sovereign move of God for the purpose of restoring truth to Christ's Church. If these seven principles are evident, then a move can rightly be called a Restoration Movement and not just a temporary spiritual renewal, or the emphasis and activity of a few people.

All of the movements mentioned in the previous chapters manifested these seven characteristics.

(1) Divine enlightenment and revelation knowledge of the truth.

(2) The occasional individual vs. the consistent company.

(3) New anointing and authority for establishing truth.

(4) A small beginning in an insignificant place.

(5) Power to reproduce by teaching, training, activating and maturing the saints.

(6) Practiced and publicized until contested and controversial.

(7) New songs, choruses and other music portraying the restoration message.

81

Here we will be concerned in particular with the way in which the Prophetic Movement displays the characteristics of a true restoration movement.

(1) DIVINE ENLIGHTENMENT AND REVELATION KNOWLEDGE OF THE TRUTH.

A truly Holy Spirit-inspired movement will bring enlightenment of certain scriptures that reveal truths and practices which were lost during the Dark Ages of the Church and which have not been properly understood and practiced since the days of the early Church. The spirit of revelation in the knowledge of Christ's timely purpose for His Church will begin to enlighten and inspire ministers to proclaim these new insights and divine activities. This causes the Church to experience new life-giving truth and to move into new ministry that it had previously not known how to receive or manifest (Eph.1:17,18; 3:1-5).

The Prophetic Movement has brought and continues to bring divine enlightenment and revelation knowledge with regard to the scriptures that reveal that God is raising up a company of prophets that will fulfill Malachi 4:5 and Isaiah 40:3-5 corporately in the same way John the Baptist fulfilled them as an individual prophet (Mt.11:9-14; 17:11). The Prophetic Movement is bringing understanding to Christendom that there are Christian prophets in our day. Teaching is going forth in churches, seminars and conferences; audio cassette tapes and videos are being produced and books are being written to spread this knowledge to the ends of the world.

Prophets are teaching and demonstrating God's purpose for restoring His ascension gift of prophet. Revelation knowledge is coming forth revealing God's purpose for raising up a company of thousands of prophets in these last days. Times and places are being made available for the teaching, training, activating and maturing of those who are called to be prophets.

Martin Luther. This first restoration movement principle of bringing revelation knowledge and illuminated scriptural understanding of a forgotten truth was established in the first major restoration movement, the Protestant Movement. The prophet that God used to bring this revelation knowledge was a young Catholic priest who taught in a small, insignificant university and pastored the local church. The more the young prophet studied and taught the Scriptures, the more frustrated he became with himself, God, the Church hierarchy and the religious system of His day. He developed an insatiable desire to know God in such a way as to have divine peace and assurance in his heart.

Although Martin Luther was a religious college graduate, a professor of religion and an ordained priest in his denomination, he still did not know how to receive a born-again experience. He did not have peace with God nor did he have any assurance that he would go directly to heaven when he died. He had done everything his church order taught to make himself holy and at peace with God.

He had lived the monastic life for years. He had practiced extreme asceticism, even to the extent of self-flagellation, endless fastings and almost anything he could think of to inflict self-punishment. This type of self-denial and penance was guaranteed by the Catholic church to bring peace with God.

Luther became frustrated with a hard-hearted and tyrannical God who demanded so much and gave so little in return. His superior had suggested that if Luther gave himself to the study of the Scriptures, perhaps he could find his peace with God. It was the best advice he ever received from his church leaders.

The Scriptures Come Alive. After years of endless study and even teaching of the Scriptures, the spirit of revelation came. Scriptures he had meditated on for years suddenly came alive with new meaning and experiential reality. Romans 1:17 and 5:1, Ephesians 2:8,9 and Titus 3:5 took on new revelation and application for Luther and became the foundational truths of the Protestant Movement.

All restoration movements start by God sovereignly giving a person a supernatural spiritual experience which causes him to understand a scriptural truth. We must grasp this truth from Luther's personal experience and testimony:

I greatly longed to understand Paul's Epistle to the Romans, and nothing stood in the way but that one expression, 'the righteousness of God,' because I took it to mean that righteousness whereby God is righteous and deals righteously in punishing the unrighteous. Night and day I pondered until...I grasped the truth that the righteousness of God is that righteousness whereby, through grace and sheer mercy, he justifies us by faith. Thereupon I felt myself to be reborn and to have gone through open doors into paradise. The whole Scriptures took on a new meaning, and whereas before 'the righteousness of God' had filled me with hate, now it became to me inexpressibly sweet in greater love. This passage of Paul became to me a gateway to heaven. (**Eerdman's Handbook to the History of Christianity**, Grand Rapids, William B. Eerdman Publishing Co., 1977; "Reform," by James Atkinson, p. 366.)

A man with a biblically-founded spiritual experience is never at the mercy of religious leaders with religious tradition and doctrines of men. Luther preached his newly-found truth and experience until it caused a great controversy within the Church. He loved his church denomination and wanted it to believe and receive the same peace and life-giving experience that he had received. Jesus used the wineskin analogy to show the futility of trying to put Christianity into Judaism: "You cannot put new wine into an old wineskin, for it will ferment and grow until it bursts the old dried and non-flexible wineskin" (Lk.5:37). Luther found out the hard way that this lesson also applied to putting Protestant truth into Catholicism.

Old Wineskins Will Not Work. You cannot put new restoration truth and experience into an old denomination with their doctrines set like cement and their articles of acceptable Christian experiences and practices—just as dry, hard and non-adjustable as an old dried goat skin that has had old wine in it for years. In five hundred years of numerous restoration movements there is no record of any of the major denominations who were established from a previous truth ever incorporating the next restored truth and practices into their articles of faith and practice. In fact, history has proven that those who were persecuted for participating in a restoration movement become the main persecutors of the next truth-restoring movement.

The religious system never changes, though many of its ministers do move into the new truth. When a movement is at its peak, everyone who becomes exposed to it will either participate or persecute. It is hard to be neutral or a secret disciple. Luther was declared a heretic and his teachings heresy by his denominational hierarchy. He was excommunicated from his church and had to flee for his life.

New Applications of Restored Truth. Not only will a restoration movement reactivate truth that has been hidden and inactive; it will bring new enlightenment and applications for truths which have already been restored. For instance, Luther received restorational revelation knowledge on how to pray to God properly. It was revealed to him that you did not need to go through priests to reach God, repeat memorized words while touching prayer beads, or pray with prayer books.

Instead, Luther learned, a person could pray directly to God in repentant prayer and receive forgiveness of sins and answers to prayers without priests, Mary, penance or any other religious requirement except faith and grace. His initial restoring revelation on prayer brought it back to its proper biblical foundation, but each movement since that time has added new insight and ability in the methods, purpose and power of prayer. The same is true for every spiritual experience in the fruits and gifts of the Holy Spirit, ministries and worship. It is also true for the six major doctrines of Christ, four of which have been restored in experiential reality and two which will surely come into experiential reality during God's coming times of restoration.

(2) THE OCCASIONAL INDIVIDUAL VS. THE CONSISTENT COMPANY.

A restoration movement will change a truth, scriptural experience or ministry from being an occasional happening for a few into a consistent practice of the thousands who participate. For instance, prior to the Pentecostal Movement, some holiness ministers and individual Christians received the spiritual experience while in prayer of speaking in a tongue that they had never learned. They called it spiritual utterances, intercessory prayer groanings or spiritual ecstasy. They knew it felt good and made Jesus more real to them but they had no idea what had happened to them, what to call it or whether others could receive the same experience.

When the restorational Pentecostal Movement came in 1900, however, revelation came that it was the same experience that the one hundred and twenty disciples of Jesus received on that Pentecost Day when God poured out His promised Holy Spirit. Because Jesus had promised to baptize with the Holy Spirit, Pentecostals called this experience of speaking in other tongues "the baptism of the Holy Ghost." Because of Peter's proclamation that all who repented and were baptized in the name of Jesus Christ could receive the gift of the Holy Ghost, some called it the "gift of the Holy Ghost" (Mt.3:11; Acts 1:5; 2:38).

When revelation knowledge came that it was a biblical experience and that it could be received by every Christian by seeking and believing for it, then thousands received it and have consistently received it until now millions are receiving this truth experience by faith and grace. This same principle applies to every truth that was and is being established in each movement.

The One and the Many. This principle of the **one** and the **many** is true in the Prophetic Movement as well. Church historians have referred to Luther and other restorational leaders as "prophets." But their contemporaries did not call them prophets, nor did they think of themselves as prophets. It was not until

1948 during the Latter Rain Movement that revelation knowledge and teaching came that there are apostles and prophets in the Church today.

A few men such as William Branham were recognized and occasionally called a prophet by their contemporaries. But there was just an occasional one here and there. Many were manifesting the gifts of healing and words of knowledge in the **deliverance evangelism** part of the movement. There were prophets in the **Latter Rain Movement**, but the only one I heard called a prophet regularly by his peers was David Schoch. In this movement they practiced their new revelation of the laying on of hands and prophecy to individuals. Within the congregations there were consistent manifestations of the gift of prophecy. The spirit and gift of prophecy were fully restored.

But the **office of the prophet** was still the **occasional one**. Even those who received and taught that there are prophets in the Church did not have the faith and freedom to identify a man as such. They would introduce a minister as "Evangelist" or "Pastor So-and-So," but not "Prophet So-and-So." The Prophetic Movement is bringing understanding, acceptance and recognition of a company of prophets that God is raising up in the Church. They are freely introducing those who have proven to be prophets and apostles as such. We introduce a speaker at our conferences as Prophet Webster, Prophetess Painter, or Apostle Anderson as easily and freely as others introduce Pastor Smith or Evangelist Graham.

Many prophets have arisen in the 80's and many more will come forth in the 90's. The principle of the "one and the many" is thus working mightily in the Prophetic Movement. Prophets will soon be so numerous and consistent in ministry that they will be as commonly accepted as pastors.

(3) NEW ANOINTING AND AUTHORITY FOR ESTABLISHING TRUTH.

The greatest anointing is upon those pioneering present truth. The greatest force of God's presence is on the crest of the wave of God's truth being restored. God gives special authority and anointing to those who will pay the price to go outside the camp of status-quo Christianity to establish a new ministry He wants activated into His Church.

They receive more of the spirit of revelation in the knowledge of Christ in His timely purposes. New wisdom and authority is granted to propagate and establish restoration truths and ministries within the Church. Additional grace is given to endure and adjust to the conflicts, controversies and persecution that come from old-order movements.

Restoration ministers are supernaturally enabled to perform signs and wonders for the confirmation of the truth preached. Worship and praise takes on new excitement. Enlightenment comes, revealing new ways of worship and new purposes for praising God. New choruses are written with different melodies conveying the truths being restored. New expressions of worship are added which are different enough from those of past movements to cause them to criticize and initially reject them. And the greatest joy, excitement and spiritual enthusiasm are among those proclaiming and participating in the present truth being restored.

(4) A SMALL BEGINNING IN AN INSIGNIFICANT PLACE.

Most restoration movements start in some insignificant obscure place. Jesus, who headed up the "New Testament Church Movement," was born in a stable in the small town of Bethlehem. Out of the millions of people on planet earth, less than a dozen people knew anything significant had happened.

It was some forty years later that Luke recorded the birth of Jesus and made it a significant historical happening that others could read about. The little baby Jesus was born of Mary, not in an expensive hospital room nor even a hotel room, but in a barn, and He was placed in that little animal feeding trough called a manger. Yet that event was the birthing of the "Messiah Movement." This established the pattern for the birthing of all future spiritual restoration movements within the Church.

I spent twenty-five years in research and three years in

writing the book *The Eternal Church*, which covers the two thousand years of Church history. I studied and researched every revival and movement I could find that people have recorded down through the years. This principle of the small beginning in an insignificant place was consistent.

Years of Preparation. The process is similar as well: God prepares a man with years of discipline and development for his day of responsibility in this area. Like a woman pregnant with a child, the truth is conceived in the womb of his spirit and then it grows over the years until there is time for birth. He goes into spiritual labor pains and the ministry is birthed into the Church.

A restoration movement progresses as Jesus did. From the cradle till He was thirty years old, Jesus was only known by a few. But when God's time for public proclamation came, then the "Jesus the Messiah Movement" became a national issue, causing conflict, confusion and great controversy within the established religious world of Judaism.

Protestant Beginnings. We should examine further this principle of "small beginnings in insignificant places" and the historical principle of establishing the official time and place that the movement is birthed into the Church and begins to be made known to the world. The Protestant Movement is known as the beginning of the period of the great restoration. This period began with one movement, but it is destined to have continuing restoration movements until the Church comes unto the full stature of Christ in character, power and purpose.

Protestant church historians have recorded October 31, 1517, as the official day the Protestant Movement was launched. But if you had been an average citizen or church member at that time and place, you would not have been aware that anything significant had happened that day. The event would not have even made the daily news, or if it had, it would probably have been a few lines on a back page like this:

Martin Luther, priest of the little Castle Church here in Wittenburg, Germany, was seen using a hammer on the door of his church before the morning service. Upon examination it was found that he had nailed a document to the door containing a list of what he believes to be ninety-five unscriptural practices and beliefs of his own denomination, the Roman Catholic Church. Very few even noticed it was there but it is reported that someone was seen making copies of the document.

It seemed to be just an insignificant happening in an obscure little place, but when copies of his "Ninety-Five Theses" began to surface in the castles of German Princes, seminaries, the religious hierarchy and even the Pope's chambers in Rome, Luther's words produced the greatest conflict and controversy ever in Christendom.

The Lutheran Church Begins. It was several years later before Luther came out of the Catholic church. But when he did, he inspired many other priests to come out as well and start independent churches.

Luther had written many books and pamphlets concerning his revelations and convictions dealing with the Scriptures and with the unscriptural practices of his denomination. Because those who started independent churches followed Luther's writings and doctrines, they were called "Lutheran" churches. In 1529 some German princes made a formal protest to the Catholic church hierarchy for condemning Luther's teachings as heresy. It split the German states into northern Protestants and southern Catholics. Those who followed Luther's teachings were called protesters and their heresies and rebellion were known as the "Protestant" religion.

A Predestined Time and Place. Within this principle lies another characteristic of Church restoration movements. God ordains many years of preparation by numerous people until His predestined time and place for launching are manifested. For instance, over a century before John Huss had propagated some of the same teachings as Luther and had sought to bring reform to his church. But he was tried by the church leaders, declared a heretic, and burned at the stake in the churchyard.

Other reformers arose as well, seeking to bring changes. At the time a restoration movement is brought forth there are usually several men of God teaching and ministering the same truths. But the principle of Church restoration and spiritual movements is that **someone** at **some time** in **some insignificant place** must be used to **launch what God wants activated**.

This does not mean the minister chosen to be the instrument is more righteous or the place more favored. It simply means that God prepares a man, a place and a time for the launching of His purpose for restoring truth and ministry into His Church. After the movement is launched, then someone studies and evaluates what happened and determines the time, place and incident that seemed to be used by God as the key action that opened the door for that movement to go out and be exposed to all Christendom and the world.

The same principles, practices and characteristic traits have been involved in every restoration movement recorded by Church historians over the last five hundred years.

Birth of the Pentecostal Movement. Some Pentecostal Movement historians have recorded December 31, 1900, as the birthday of their movement. The place was Topeka, Kansas, at the Reverend Charles Fox Parham's Bible School. The incident or setting that birthed it was a watch-night prayer service.

The immediate preparation was that the faculty and students had been studying that school semester to determine the consistent biblical evidence for the "baptism of the Holy Ghost." They all concluded it was the "unknown tongues." They laid hands on a student at her request, and to their surprise she received a supernatural ability to speak in a tongue unknown to her and to those present. That was the beginning of the revelation for application and activation of twentieth century Christians into the baptism of the Holy Spirit.

Other Pentecostal historians whose denominational roots did not come from Topeka, Kansas, give the great Azusa Street Revival that began in Los Angeles in 1906 as the birthday of the Pentecostal Movement. Both are applicable. Topeka was the time and place where the revelation came that people could receive the baptism of the Holy Spirit with speaking in other tongues as a deliberate act of faith. The event was thus taken out of the realm of "God's sovereign choice only" to the realm of "whosoever will may believe and receive." In other words, you could set a time and place, then believe and pray for people to receive the Holy Spirit gift with speaking in tongues.

But the revelation did not immediately spread to all the world from Topeka. Instead, one black preacher who had been influenced by them, Reverend William Seymour, went to Los Angeles and started meetings at an insignificant place on Azusa Street. There a Pentecostal revival started that ran continuously for three years. People came from all over the world to discover what new thing God had wrought. It became the center for a multiplication of the movement around the world.

Numerous books are available that give pages of personal testimony from those who were present at these services. Some give extensive details concerning the setting, the prior preparation and the people involved. It is very enlightening and interesting reading. My purpose here in giving just a few condensed examples of restoration movements being birthed is to reveal the principle that they begin at an insignificant place with a small beginning with very few people (comparatively speaking) knowing that anything significant is happening at the time.

THE BEGINNINGS OF THE PROPHETIC MOVEMENT

The Prophetic Movement has followed the typical restorational pattern with regard to its beginnings. As with other restorational movements, prior to its birth there had been a progressive work going on for years in the lives of many people, with several years of revelation, preparation and application.

Many were pregnant with this movement for years before it was birthed into the Church.

My own role in the movement began when God first revealed to me that I was called as a prophet, through the words of the prophetic presbytery in 1953 (described in the previous chapter and in the preface of *Prophets and Personal Prophecy*). The seed revelation concerning the ministry of end-time prophets in the Church was placed in my spirit at that time. For several years I preached that specific revelation quite often while I ministered as an individual prophet.

Schools of the Holy Spirit. But my work in the calling forth, training and activating of prophets and a prophetic people did not start until some twenty-five years later. God gave me a commission in 1979 to start "Schools of the Holy Spirit" for activating Spirit-filled saints into their gifts of the Holy Spirit, thereby enabling them to become a prophetic people.

After *The Eternal Church* was published in 1981, God began to talk to me more about the great company of prophets He would bring forth in the 1980's and 90's. I had already been ministering to thousands over the years in personal prophecy. Since numerous other prophets were going to arise doing the same thing, some books desperately needed to be written giving guidelines for giving and receiving personal prophecies. And both the prophets and the prophesying saints needed to be taught and trained how to minister both in spirit and word.

At that time I began to receive numerous prophecies from my peer prophets that I was to write the book I was telling others needed to be written. I gathered research materials, insights and experiences for the book, and began writing the manuscript, a process which was to take several years.

Meanwhile, as I started on the book, God began to give me a greater burden and vision for prophets and the prophetic ministry. So we started conducting prophets conferences in the fall of that year, 1982. We continued the local Friday night School of the Holy Spirit during this time.

Then in 1984 God directed us to move the headquarters of

Christian International to the panhandle of Florida. There, we started having prophets seminars quarterly, then bimonthly, and then every six weeks. During this same time we were conducting prophet conferences throughout the United States and several foreign countries as well. We have now conducted over fifty prophets seminars and conferences.

The book *Prophets and Personal Prophecy* was finally published in September 1987. Now in its fifth printing, totalling 50,000 copies in print. But even then I realized that all that needed to be said on this subject could not be covered in one book. So a series of four volumes was planned, including the present one.

Prophetic Labor Pains. We were pregnant with this ministry for quite some time. When a woman is pregnant with a baby she carries it nine months, but when a man of God is pregnant with a vision that is destined to become a restorational movement in the Church, he carries it for years. Labor pains can begin one year without the birth taking place till a year later.

Our beginning labor pains came at Christian International's first National Prophets Conference near Destin, Florida. (As far as I can determine by historical research, it was the first national prophets conference ever conducted in the history of the Church). Over seven hundred attended this gathering. On Friday, October 23, 1987—the third night of the conference—God moved in a sovereign sweep of His Spirit at 10:00 PM in the evening. A spirit of intercessory warfare prayer-praise arose spontaneously within all the people, and for the next forty-five minutes there was a heavenly warfare in the Spirit like few have ever witnessed.

Visions and prophecies were given by many of those present, revealing what had just transpired. The main emphasis of the words given was that the battle had been won for the release and activation of the great company of prophets that God had pre-ordained to be raised up in this century and even at this very time. The sovereign move of God in that service was the preliminary labor pains that placed the "baby" prophetic movement in proper position along the "birth canal" for "delivery" the following year.

The Birth of the Prophetic Movement. One year later, the second CI-NPM International Prophets Conference was meeting in the ballroom of the Sandestin Beach Resort Inn in Sandestin, Florida, just fifteen miles west of the CI campus. It was October 15, 1988, the third night of the conference. At 10:15 PM, when I had finished preaching on God's purpose for His great company of prophets being brought forth, a spirit of travail arose within me, and a mighty anointing swept over me as I began to travail in spiritual birth. The same spirit swept throughout the audience of over eight hundred, and for the next fifty minutes most of us travailed in prophetic intercessory prayer.

This intensified in my spirit until I felt my soul was being torn out as we cried out in the travail of birth pangs. I almost physically passed out from the intensity of the anointing and spiritual birth pangs. Finally, my whole body felt "weak as water," as if my very life was going out of me.

I crumpled to my knees and was immediately caught up in the Spirit. Then I saw a vision of God lifting me and many others to a higher realm. He gave me a vision of the thousands of prophets He was bringing forth at this time.

A New Baby. This company of prophets was in the hand of God like a baby which had just been brought from the womb. He asked if I would be one of those who would help raise up what He had birthed. He stated that a new anointing and authority had been granted for this purpose and that all who were there and those around the world who had received His vision for the company of prophets would receive that same anointing.

As I ascended up with Him in the Spirit, all those present ascended also and began to form into a structure that would propagate the prophetic. I looked and saw other structures arising all over the world. He said this was the structure He had given me and that the others were many other prophetic groups that He is raising up. I was to work to help bring unity, relationship and a networking among the different camps of prophets.

Christ's Company of Prophets. God revealed other things that night as well about His purpose for prophets. But what I want to emphasize here is that those present sensed the revelational reality that an official decree had been given in heaven for the activation and proclamation of Christ's company of prophets. Some of these prophets had been in progressive preparation for many years; others had been hidden away in the wilderness like the prophet Moses. Many prophets were just now coming forth.

This company would now begin to be manifest upon the earth. They were to lead God's people out of religious bondage and give prophetic proclamations to national leaders and systems, saying, "Let God's people go!"

The Prophetic "Blast-Off." The "launching pad" of preparation and the "space shuttle" of the Prophetic Movement had been in a state of preparation for years for God's appointed time for launching. The countdown had begun several years before, and finally progressed to the moment of blast-off.

Time and History Will Tell. Being a church historian, I know that only time and history can determine the factual reality of a prophetic revelation and declaration. I am thoroughly convinced by God's divine visitation and all that I have received from Christ that October 15, 1988, was the launching of the prophetic for myself and the CI-NPM into a prophetic movement. That night I surrendered unconditionally to Christ Jesus as I received the commission from Him to take a responsible role in God's purpose for His company of prophets which are to personify Him and to perpetuate His divine purpose for His Church on planet earth.

Only time and history will reveal whether one of the divine Church restoration principles was at work that night: **SOMEONE at SOME INSIGNIFICANT PLACE must be used to LAUNCH what GOD wants ACTIVATED.** I personally believe that God's timely purpose for His prophets was officially birthed into the Church world on October 15, 1988, and was launched into what has become known in the 1990's as the Prophetic Movement.

It was a successful launching, and the Prophetic Movement is now orbiting around God's eternal purpose for His Church and for planet earth. God has purposed that the prophets will continue to grow in number, maturity and power until they fulfill their purpose of **"making ready a people"** and **"preparing the way"** for the return of Christ as King of Kings and Lord of Lords (Is.40:3-5; Lk.1:17).

We had never had a service like that before, nor have we had one since. You cannot by faith or practice generate a sovereign move of the Holy Spirit like that; you can only flow with it when it comes. I have checked with other major prophets around the world and they also experienced some sovereign visitations and revelations from God that brought confirmation and agreement that the launching of the company of prophets and birthing of the Prophetic Movement was in 1988.

Forty Years. An interesting time element of forty years is involved here. It was in 1947—forty years before the initial "labor pains" in our conference—that William Branham, Paul Cain and a few other men arose as prophets within the Church. But they were just the few, and they began to fade from public ministry for awhile.

Then, it was on February 14, 1948, that the Latter Rain Movement was supernaturally birthed at a small gathering of about seventy ministers and Bible school students in North Battleford, Saskatchewan, Canada. The particular truth restored at that time was the teaching and practice of personal prophecy to individuals by prophets and the prophetic presbytery, and the revelation knowledge that there are apostles and prophets in the twentieth-century Church. The movement started in a small, insignificant place, but within a few years it had spread across the world. In the 50's it caused a great controversy among Pentecostal churches.

It was exactly forty years from 1948 to 1988—between the Latter Rain Movement, which revealed that there are prophets, and the Prophetic Movement, which revealed and proclaimed that God wants to bring forth at this time a great company of prophets. It was forty years from the time that Moses personally received the desire to deliver God's people from Egyptian slavery until the time that he led the whole company of Israelites out of Egypt. He first came out of Egypt as an individual prophet, but forty years later he came out with a multitude of God's prophetic people (Num.11:29).

Faithful Prophets During 40 Year Period. During this period several prophetic ministers, such as, John and Paula Sanford, Kenneth Hagin, Frank Damazio and scores of others from various charismatic groups, wrote books about prophets and the prophetic ministry.

Prophets from the Restoration camp, such as David Schoch, Emanuele Cannistraci and others, not only participated in prophetic presbyteries but personally prophesied to hundreds of individuals. The few I have mentioned represent only the "tip of the iceberg" of unheralded prophets who have faithfully maintained the prophetic ministry over the years.

Other Prophetic Ministries. While God was birthing His purposes in Christian International, the Holy Spirit was working to raise up other groups to further propagate the prophetic. Grace Ministries in Kansas City, Missouri, began to gain prominence as a prophetic ministry in the late 80's with such prophetic ministers as Mike Bickle, Bob Jones and John Paul Jackson. Other prophets like Bernard Jordan of Zoe Ministries in Brooklyn, New York; Rick Joyner of Charlotte, North Carolina; Glenn Foster of Sweetwater Church in Phoenix, Arizona; Dick Mills of Hemet, California; Kim Clements and Eddie Traut of South Africa; and the members of the Ohio Prophetic Association and many others around the world began to major in manifesting and propagating the prophetic ministry.

Perhaps the most prominent of these is Paul Cain of Dallas,

Texas. According to Paul's personal testimony, it was in 1987, after twenty-five years of restricted ministry, that he was allowed by the Lord to return to his full prophetic ministry. Paul had been used mightily in the Healing Movement of the 40's and 50's, but God had told him to pull away from the corruption and self-promotion that was developing in many circles.

Paul Cain states that the Lord told him that there would be a new breed of men and women of God who would arise in the last days, and they would not yield to such temptations. When this great company began to be manifested, he would be re-activated in public ministry again. This began to take place in 1988. The time for the manifestation of that company has come, and Paul Cain's ministry is blossoming again in prophetic power.

Both the True and False are Signs of the Times. Jesus declared that one of the great signs of the end times would be the arising of many false Christs, false teachers and especially false prophets (Mt.24:24; 2Cor.11:13; 2Pet.2:1). Some will be proclaimed as prophets, and some groups will claim to be prophetic, but will not necessarily be ordained of God. False prophets and false prophetic groups will arise in the 1990's. However, this only gives greater proof to the validity of God's true company of prophets. For there cannot be a false Christ, unless there is truly a real Christ—no false prophets unless there are God ordained true prophets. There could be no counterfeit money unless there is government authorized money in circulation. Christians must make sure that they do not reject the true prophets because of an encounter with a false prophet, prophecy or prophetic ministry.

The Prophets Are God's Great End-Time Sign. Dispensational theologians and Israel-oriented preachers were looking for the Lord to come in 1988 because it would be forty years from the time Israel was made a state in May of 1948. One of them even wrote a book giving the eighty-eight reasons why Jesus would come in 1988. But sadly enough, those who try to interpret every significant happening in the events concerning natural

Israel to determine the timing of the second coming of Jesus miss some of the great spiritual things God has done and is doing in His Church.

The greatest sign of the nearness of the second coming of Jesus Christ back to earth actually did happen in 1988. It was the birthing of the Prophetic Movement. But many failed to recognize the sign.

When prophet John the Baptist was brought forth in the spirit of Elijah, it was the greatest sign ever given that the Messiah was at hand: The generation that was alive when prophet John started his "Elijah" ministry was the same generation that was alive when Jesus was manifested, died, rose again and established His Church on earth. Yet the leading theologians of that day and hour could not perceive it as a sign at all because they were looking for a literal Elijah and a literal fulfillment of the Messiah as a conquering King rather than a suffering Savior.

If the "first shall be last and the last first," then perhaps the last coming of Christ will be like His first coming. If this is true, then the present-day Church should rejoice—for the generation that is alive now, with the company of prophets who are coming forth in the spirit of Elijah, will be the ones to see the second coming of Jesus and the establishing of His Kingdom on earth as it is in heaven. We should lift up our heads and rejoice, for our redemption draweth nigh! (Mk.10:31; Mt.6:10;16:28; Lk.21:28).

(5) POWER TO REPRODUCE BY TEACHING, TRAINING, ACTIVATING AND MATURING THE SAINTS.

Every true restoration movement not only has the previous four aspects, but also is characterized by a fifth: It gives men and women the revelation and power to reproduce in others the ministry God has birthed in them.

The Reproduction Principle. In the creation of all living things God established the law that everything was to reproduce after its kind. Every seed was to reproduce another plant or animal which had the power to reproduce another of the same, and on and on the cycle was to go (see Gen.1:1-2:25).

Every true ministry which is restored in the movement is designed, not just to make the ministry known, but to reproduce after its kind. The *revelation* of a restoration truth is only a *seed*. The **movement** that brings wisdom and anointing **for** *reproducing* the restored ministry **is the** *mature plant* ready for harvesting its seeds and reproducing itself.

Seeds Must Go Through a Process. A seed cannot produce another seed directly. It must produce a body or plant, which then produces another seed. For instance, a grain of corn does not duplicate itself into another grain of corn. Instead, it must be planted into the ground, die to itself and allow the new corn plant life to germinate, sprout, grow to a great corn stalk, produce a pollinating tassel and ear of corn and then maintain a maturing process until that corn has ripened sufficiently to become **"seed corn"** for reproducing more corn.

That is why leaders of movements must have been in preparation for years before they are qualified to be launched into a reproducing ministry. That is why those who have just received the seed of revelation of the restored truth are not able to reproduce after their kind until God takes them through the process. They can be an example of what a prophet is and demonstrate the prophetic seed ministry, but they will not have the vision, wisdom, anointing or maturity to reproduce other prophetic seeds.

Those who are not willing to die to self and go through the transforming process of growing into maturity develop counterfeit methods of manufacturing seeds. They may look the same as the true, natural seed, but they do not have the self-germinating life that only God can put in a seed. These counterfeit prophets are not willing to pay the price of going through the process. They want a short-cut to success.

Non-Reproductive Prophetic Ministers. Jude 11-12 calls these ministers Balaam-type prophets—clouds without rain and dead trees who cannot produce fruit with reproductive seeds. Jude says their motive for ministering is reward rather than reproducing the ministry in others. Their prophetic ministry has a form of godliness but it does not have the power to reproduce (2Tim.3:5).

They are motivated by a love for self-acceptance, power and promotion rather than the agape love of 1 Corinthians 13, which is serving others and not serving self. Paul says they sound like prophets but they are "sounding brass and tinkling cymbals" (1Cor.13:1).

We must learn to discern the true prophets. We will know them by their fruit with seed that is able to reproduce the same ministry in others. The spirit and vision of the true prophet is to reproduce prophetic people and not just to reap the prophet's reward.

Protestant Movement Reproducers. Protestant reformers received the revelation of being born again. They published thousands of books and articles to bring forth the revelation. But it was the next movement, that of the Evangelical Baptists and others, who aggressively sought to make born-again believers out of all who would receive the revelation.

They scripturally taught people how to be born again and led them in a sinner's prayer; thereby birthing them into the Kingdom. They activated the gift of eternal life within them and then taught them how to demonstrate that new life and to reproduce it in others. Counterfeit Christian groups such as the Jehovah's Witnesses will seemingly do the same, but they are not reproducing by the Spirit of God; they are manufacturing and duplicating by artificial means.

Latter Rain Was the Seed. The 1948 Latter Rain Movement brought the seed of revelation that there are prophets in the Church today, but the 1988 Prophetic Movement is bringing the activation and reproducing of those prophets. The seed was planted in the Church forty years ago, and by 1988 it had matured to the place that it was ready to be reaped and launched into a reproducing Prophetic Movement.

Those prophets who came forth in the late 1940's were

great demonstrators of the office of prophet. Several of those prophets received visions that there would be a whole company of prophets brought forth before the coming of the Lord. Most of those did not live to see that day, but their visions were true and are coming to pass.

The Vision of Reproduction is Misunderstood. Training and activation in prophetic ministry is a primary goal of the CI-NPM. Consequently, this group has probably propagated the reproductive principle more than any other prophetic organization. For the same reason, however, its vision has often been misunderstood or rejected.

Those who question or reject the training of prophetic ministers usually fall into one of several categories. First are those prophetic leaders who have their roots in the previous moves of God during the latter decades of this century. Those who are descendants of these earlier movements are often still under the impression that prophets are one of a kind and cannot reproduce after their kind. They do not understand how those who are propagating the Prophetic Movement can reproduce prophetic ministry in others.

The second group is traditional Pentecostals. Most Pentecostal denominations did not even accept the "seed" revelation of the Latter Rain Movement that there are Church prophets today. So it is doubtful that they will be able to accept the Prophetic Movement either, which propagates the teaching, training and activating of those called to be prophets and the making of saints into prophetic people.

Most Charismatics have not been sufficiently exposed to prophetic ministry by either doctrine or demonstration to come to any conclusions about accepting or rejecting, participating or persecuting. Their response as a whole is yet to be seen.

A Clarification of Terms. This series will include a separate volume on how to train prophets, produce a prophetic people and grow prophetic ministers. To avoid misunderstanding, however, it might be useful at this point to clarify what we mean by this. We do **not** believe that anyone can make others be and do what God has not called them to be and do. But we **can** teach, train and activate them to do and be what God has called them to do and be.

I cannot, for example, make someone a Christian unless the Holy Spirit draws that person to Christ. I cannot educate and activate people into eternal life unless they believe, receive and then live the Christian life themselves.

Nevertheless, all evangelicals would agree that Christians can give sinners the saving knowledge of Jesus Christ, lead them in a sinner's prayer and allow them to believe in their heart and confess with their mouth that Jesus is Lord. Those ministering can then declare upon the authority of God's Word and the response to it that those being ministered to have been born again, that they have the gift of eternal life, and that they have been translated from the kingdom of darkness and activated into the kingdom of God's dear Son. The new believers can then by God's grace and biblical faith principles draw upon the attributes of that new divine life to overcome the world, flesh and the devil.

Evangelical Christians who minister in this way reproduce other Christians. They take sinners and make them saints—by teaching, training and activating them to do and become what God has called them to do and become.

Divine Principles are Consistent. By following the same biblical principles we can take average Spirit-filled Christians and make them into productive prophetic people. We can take average ministers and make them powerful prophetic ministers, maturing them to the place of reproducing their kind. And we can recognize those called by God to be prophets, then train them to function in their calling with maturity and wisdom.

A Reproducer of Reproducers. This ministry of being a reproducer was prophesied to me by one of my peer prophets—in fact, one of the few prophets I know who is older than I am in age and years as a prophet. The following is an excerpt from a prophecy delivered to me by Prophet Leland Davis on March 12, 1984, in Phoenix, Arizona, during a prophets conference:

> Dr. Hamon, the Lord showed me something about you when I first met you. He showed me that the heart cry within you was for unity within the Body of Christ and to see one Church, just the whole Body of Christ flowing together. You have fought long and hard for that and He is going to let you get in on the benefits of seeing some things come together.... You are going to bring forth revelation for the activating of the Body of Christ into the gifts of the Holy Spirit. There is going to be a whole **new wave** of God's glory that is going to be ignited through your ministry... and it's going to be the multiplying of yourself, for you are to have a ministry of **producing reproducers who will reproduce reproducers that also will reproduce reproducers.**... And the knitting together in this situation is going to take place in the next five years.

Only The Godhead Can Give Gifts. It should go without saying that Christ Jesus is the **only** one who can call someone to a fivefold ministry of apostle, prophet, evangelist, pastor or teacher. I am a reproducing apostolic-prophet minister, but if God has not called a person to be a prophet, no matter how much I educate, activate and prophesy over that person, I cannot make a prophet out of him or her.

God has given this ability only to Christ Jesus. **He alone** "gives gifts to men, some apostles and some prophets..." (Eph. 4:11). **God alone** has "set in the Church apostles and prophets" (1Cor.12:28) and God has "set the members in the Body as it pleases Him" (1Cor.12:18).

If **God**, however, has **called a person** to be a **prophet,** then I can **educate, activate, motivate and mature** that **calling** into the **commissioning** of a **prophet** in the Body of Christ. Elijah, for example, took Elisha—whom God had called to be a prophet— and brought him through the process for about eleven years, until he had educated, activated and reproduced another prophet of like kind who even did twice as many miracles as he had. A senior pastor can do the same with a person who has the ascension gift and calling to be a pastor.

Every pastor of a church or head of a ministry needs to have those of like calling and vision being prepared to carry on the ministry. Moses had Joshua in training for forty years to reproduce after his kind. The Apostle Paul produced another apostle in Timothy (2Tim.2:2).

Prophets Training Prophets. Samuel was the senior prophet who had the vision for starting schools of the prophets throughout Israel. He headquartered in Ramah and traveled to cities like Gilgal, Jericho and others where he had established training centers for prophets.

Other prophets such as Elijah and Elisha continued this senior prophet ministry to the prophets in Israel. At times the senior prophet would send one of the "sons of the prophets" to deliver the word of the Lord to someone, as when Elisha sent one of his young prophets to deliver a prophecy to General Jehu and to anoint him for his kingship ministry. Today there are places being raised up in a similar way for the schooling of prophets. These training centers are activating them into their calling and training to become pure and mature New Testament Church prophets.

(6) PRACTICED AND PUBLICIZED UNTIL CONTESTED AND CONTROVERSIAL.

Within a few years after the truth has been launched within the Church through a restorational movement, it grows to national and worldwide prominence. By then it is being publicized and practiced by enough people to bring it to the attention of the leaders of independent groups of past movements.

Many of these leaders and local pastors of past movement churches begin to receive reports that their people are involved with the new movement. Their church members have started reading some of the movement's materials and attending some of its churches or conferences, and they consequently have become exposed to the teachings, with some even participating and receiving ministry there. These members then bring the information to their church and begin testifying about this new wonderful experience they received while attending the other services.

This process took place with each of the historic restoration movements. For example, with the Pentecostal and Charismatic Movements, denominational church members received the baptism of the Holy Spirit with unknown tongues. So their pastors were forced to take a stand concerning these new doctrines, practices and spiritual experiences.

Responses to the New Movement. When this occurs, some of the pastors and denominational leaders will take a neutral attitude: "Hold steady; do nothing; wait and see." Others will accept the new truths and ministries and incorporate them into their own teachings, ministry and ways of worship. But some will reject and condemn the movement.

Those who do not like the movement and want nothing to do with it will find examples of ministers or members who have been confused or hurt by their involvement in the movement to prove that it is not of God. They will also focus on little phrases or particular teachings of the leaders of the movement and make them sound unscriptural, out of order or cultic. Those who oppose and persecute the movement will declare publicly that it is not of God and forbid their members to participate. The leaders of past movement independent groups and denominations will finally issue an official document declaring that this movement is not condoned by them and is therefore not of God.

Past Movement Leaders Oppose the New. Those who were the leaders of what was God's established order until the new movement came along are the ones who fight what is new the hardest. Moses, for example, had a divine visitation on Mount Sinai that resulted in what we could call the "Tabernacle-Ceremonial Law" Movement. The religious leaders of this movement who looked to Abraham as their father were the ones that rejected and crucified the "Jesus the Messiah Movement."

God raised up Abraham to launch and establish the Jewish race. Then five hundred years later God raised up Moses to establish the dispensation of the Law for His chosen race. But during the next fifteen hundred years the children of Israel and their Jewish leaders allowed the ceremonial Law and Tabernacle worship to become deluded, perverted and deteriorated by misuse and wrong interpretation and applications. Religious leaders added their own ideas and traditions until the spirit and purpose of the Law was lost.

Origination to Deterioration. Jesus came two thousand years after the call of Abraham and fulfilled all the prophecies concerning the Messiah. He then established the Church and inspired the writing of the New Testament to reveal what the Church is in power, practice and purpose. It was a glorious, victorious Church during its first century, but gradually over the next fifteen hundred years religious leaders did the same thing to the Church that former leaders did to God's glorious Law and Tabernacle.

The true Church began to be buried beneath the additions of religious men's ideas and traditions. All of the truths and supernatural experiences that the first-century Church believed and practiced were lost except those contained in the Apostles' Creed. The first three centuries of the Church saw great growth while suffering its greatest persecution. Then for the next two centuries it became accepted and finally was made the state religion of the Roman Empire. It deteriorated into an apostate Church for the next thousand years. Jesus prophesied and the New Testament writers wrote that this situation would develop in the Church, calling it the time of the great falling away. Historians have referred to this same period of time as the Dark Ages (Mt.24:1-51; He.3:12; 2Pet.3:15-17; 2Th.2:3,10-12).

Deterioration to Restoration. The Apostle Peter gave a pro-phetic declaration that before the second coming of Jesus there would be a period of time when God would send times of refreshing, or many restoration movements (Acts 3:19). He declared that Jesus could not return until that period of restora-tional movements had fulfilled its mission (vv. 20-21).

Fifteen hundred years later, God announced in heaven that it was time for that divine prophetic decree to be activated on earth within His Church. As God raised up Moses for the giving of the Law, and Jesus to establish the Church, even so God raised up Martin Luther to launch the Church into its period of the great restoration.

I believe that restoration period is destined to last for five hundred years in order to complete the two-thousand-year period that seemingly has been ordained for the Age of the Mortal Church. This does not mean that the year A.D.2000 will fulfill that period of time, for the Church was birthed, according to our Roman calendar, in A.D.30. It will be at the earliest A.D.2030 before at least two thousand years will have tran-spired.

New Race Started Every Two Thousand Years. God's timetable for mortal humanity on earth seems to have been divided into three time periods of approximately two thousand years each. If we start with the removal of Adam and Eve from the Garden of Eden as the year 0, we can call that the year of the beginning of the mortal human race. Two thousand years later God called Abraham to father a special Hebrew race for Him that would be called out from the rest of the human race. Two thousand years after that Jesus came and fathered a new race called the sons of God, what we might call the "Church race." This race has eternal life in mortal bodies.

About two thousand years later Jesus is coming back to resurrect and translate this race into his immortal Church race of people. They will have eternal spirits in their new, eternal, immortalized, flesh-and-bone human bodies. This is the end result of the last restorational movement and the one in which every Christian wants to be a participant.

All Restoration Churches Are "Ecclesia." When Church restoration began, all of Christendom in Europe and Asia was either Eastern Orthodox or Western Catholic. Martin Luther was a Catholic priest when he received the revelation that led to the Protestant Movement. It was his Catholic church leaders that declared him a heretic and excommunicated him from their fellowship.

The Catholics had held what little light was left of Christianity for over a thousand years. They had fought against the invasion of barbarians and the onslaught of Mohammed's militant religion, Islam. But when God started restoring His Church back to its original glory, they greatly resisted and persecuted that first restoration movement. So the Protestant churches, like all restorational churches, had to become the **ecclesia**—the New Testament Greek word for "church" which literally means "called out."

The Persecuted Become the Persecutors. Later, it was the Historic Protestant Movement churches that persecuted the Anabaptist and Puritan Movements. Later still, the Baptist and Holiness churches persecuted the Pentecostal Movement. Then the Pentecostal denominations followed the same pattern of rejecting and persecuting the Latter Rain and Charismatic Movements.

In the days to come, the most recent movements—Charismatics, Faith churches and Kingdom churches—will have to take a stand with regard to the restoration of prophets and the prophetic ministry. Some will try to stay neutral by ignoring it or convincing themselves that it is not significant enough to merit their involvement. Others will embrace the benefits of the truths and experiences propagated by the new movement, incorporating them into their teachings, practices and ways of worship.

Others, however, will reject and condemn the Prophetic Movement based on bad reports and a lack of understanding or appreciation of what it is all about. Still others will agree that there are prophets and apostles in the Church today, and that God does speak and minister prophetically in the Church. But they will justify their failure to participate in the movement by insisting that they do not like some of its leaders or some of the ways that its truths and ministries are administered.

Restoration Not an Option. Nevertheless, a divine restorational truth is not an option or a matter of personal preference. It is a matter of accepting or rejecting what God is trying to reinstate back into His Church. The Holy Spirit gives allowances for a variety of ways to minister and manifest the truths, spiritual ministries and ways of worship that come with a restorational movement. But there are no variables for the basic core of what God is trying to do.

We must either accept or reject, condemn or condone, participate or persecute after we have been fully exposed to a restored truth. Our lack of interest in or neglect of the truth will not be excused. For the writer of Hebrews declares:

How shall we escape, if we neglect so great salvation; which at the first began to be spoken by the Lord, and was confirmed unto us by them that heard him; God also bearing them witness, both with signs and wonders, and with divers miracles, and gifts of the Holy Ghost [a prophetic people], according to his own will? (He.2:3,4).

How Shall We Escape if We Neglect His Will? It is God's predestinated purpose and divine will for His company of prophets to be fully restored in His Church at this time. It is His will that every Church member add the dimension of the prophetic ministry into their lives and membership ministry into the Body of Christ. It is God's will that all the fivefold ministers become prophetic ministries so that they can minister as the oracles of God with the mind of Christ for the establishing of God's saints in the present truth (1Pet.4:11; 2Pet.1:12).

All Church members need to come into the full productivity,

maturity and spiritual manifestations of their potential to fulfill their predestined purpose in Christ Jesus. This is what it means to become a prophetic people.

Persecution of the Early Church. The first apostles and prophets of the Church received their rejection and persecution from the Jewish Pharisees and Sadducees. The persecution intensified when the Apostle Paul pulled out of the "Pharisee denomination" to start an independent New Testament church at Ephesus. After that, other apostles and prophets began establishing Christian churches outside and independent of the Jewish synagogues.

In the early days the Roman Empire persecuted the disciples very little, because they did not know the difference between Jews and Christians. But when the temple in Jerusalem was destroyed in A.D.70 (forty years after the Church was birthed in A.D.30) and the Jews were dispersed, Christianity was seen by the world as a distinct group from Judaism.

Christians began ministering to Roman citizens and refusing to serve or reverence the many Roman gods. Believers preached and prophesied the word of the Lord to the Romans, and the result was millions of Christian martyrdoms at the hand of the Empire over the following two hundred years.

Persecution of the Prophetic Movement. The same will be true for the prophets and prophetic people who come forth in this prophetic movement. At the first the rejection and persecution will be only from past movement leaders within the Church. Hundreds of prophetic churches will be established during the 1990's, which will provoke the old-order ministers. This will cause a great controversy among the leaders of all the movements that have taken place in this century.

But God's purpose for prophets and a prophetic people is not just to minister in and to the Church. Persecution of the prophetic movement from the churches will peak in the mid-1990's. But then there will begin a shake-up and transition within the Church. The prophets will begin to prophesy to national leaders and to confront all false religious groups that practice super-natural spirit communication: witches, occultists, spiritualists, New Agers and even Satan worshippers.

This confrontation will bring the wrath of the world systems to bear against the prophets and apostles who will be restored by that time. In fact, the two revelatory and prophetic ministers of the New Testament Church are the apostle and the prophet. So they will both prophesy and execute judgments upon the world systems similar to those of the two prophetic witnesses described in Revelation 11:3-6:

> And I will give power unto my two witnesses, and they shall **prophesy**.... And if any man will hurt them, fire proceedeth out of their mouth, and devoureth their enemies: and if any man will hurt them, he must in this manner be killed. These have power to shut heaven, that it rain not in the days of their **prophecy**: and have power over waters to turn them to blood, and to smite the earth with all plagues, as often as they will.

The Prophetic Movement in the 1990's. The Prophetic Movement will follow this principle of a true restorational movement just like the others. It will escalate and gain international momentum in the 1990's. It will progress on through publications and electronic media until it is publicized worldwide. Then it will cause great controversy among all the "tongues-talking" churches.

The Prophetic Movement will not die, but will flow alongside the movement that will bring full restoration to the office of apostle. It will then work with all the fivefold ministers walking in present truth to equip and mature the saints. At last the Church will powerfully demonstrate the kingdom of God to the world for a final witness to them that Jesus is Lord and the only way, truth and life for humankind. Then the consummation of the ages will be climaxed in the final restorational move of the Holy Spirit and the return of Jesus as King over all the domains of earth, and Lord of the universe.

(7) NEW SONGS, CHORUSES and OTHER MUSIC POR-TRAYING THE RESTORATION MESSAGE.

During each restoration movement God brings forth those men and women who write songs and choruses with a new musical sound that melodiously manifests the message that the movement leaders are called to preach and prophesy. A thorough study of the progression of music within each movement shows that each movement has enriched the music step by step until now it involves the entire human spirit, soul and body in its expressions of praise and worship to the Lord.

Martin Luther and his fellow reformers wrote several songs during the Protestant Movement that portrayed the spirit and truth of the movement. Most singing in the Catholic church during Luther's time was sung by the monks in a monotone chant without any physical movement except their mouths. Many thought that the more serious, slow and mechanical the singing, the more holy it was to the Lord. But when Luther received his born-again experience, he was also delivered from the dead works of his lifeless, ritualistic worship.

Luther received the peace of God in his spirit and the joy of God in his soul. So the truths of his new Christian life were expressed in music with new words and melodies that some in the religious establishment thought worldly, soulish and even sacrilegious. One of the best known of these songs is Luther's great hymn, "A Mighty Fortress Is Our God."

Holiness Movement Songs. Thousands of songs were written during the three hundred years of the Holiness Movement, and we know many of them today as 'the great hymns of the Church.' Most song books used today by denominational churches are filled with the songs written during this period of time. These songs express the sovereign greatness of God, the cleansing blood of Jesus, the grace of God, Christian commitment, holiness, sacrificial living and gratefulness for God's love, mercy and blessings.

A divine restorational principle was established in Luther's time. When God raises up someone (usually an apostle or prophet) to proclaim a new restoration truth, He also raises up an anointed minstrel to write those messages into songs and choruses that express the spirit and truths of what is being restored. For example, John Wesley is known as the father of the Holiness Movement, but few people know that his brother Charles was anointed to put to music what John preached. Charles wrote over six thousand songs, four thousand of which were published.

Pentecostal Songs. The Pentecostal Movement added several new songs that talked more about the healing power and exuberant joy than the other benefits of their spiritual experience, the baptism in the Holy Spirit. They established as acceptable practice the raising of the hands in worship and clapping the hands in rhythm to the faster hymns and choruses. These two physical expressions in worship have remained and intensified with each movement since then.

The Pentecostal Movement developed during the time of the first great World War and the great Depression. There was not much joy or hope on planet earth at that time, so Pentecostals tended to have an anti-world attitude that made them long for their eternal home in heaven. The Pentecostals' typical eschatology called for an imminent return of Christ, with the "rapture" as the greatest hope and goal of the Church. So they did not often think in long-range terms; Jesus was expected to come any moment.

Consequently, many of the songs that found their way into Pentecostal hymnals were about heaven: "I'll Fly Away," "In the Sweet Bye and Bye," "Just Over in the Gloryland," "Won't It Be Wonderful There," "Will There Be Any Stars in My Crown?" Most songs either looked to what had happened in the past—"How the Old Account Was Settled Long Ago"—or what would happen in the future—"Everybody Will Be Happy Over There." Not many of them contained words that called for actions and challenges to the Church to do great things for God in the present.

To their credit, the Pentecostal Movement added all kinds

of musical instruments to their worship to accompany their singing. And they sang and shouted their praises loudly, sometimes "dancing in the Spirit" with wild abandon. Their restoration movement brought Christian singing to a new level of liberty, excitement and animated worship with more of the entire human spirit, soul and body being involved.

Latter Rain Worship. The Latter Rain Movement added the new dimension of singing praises instead of just shouting them to God. This praise was sovereignly brought forth into the Church as a melodious worship that flowed up and down like rhythmic waves or gentle breezes, then rose to a crescendo of praise that is best described by John's words in Revelation 19:6, "the sound of many waters."

Worship in these churches would continue with uplifted hands for about twenty minutes, then subside to a melodious murmur. Several prophecies would come forth, then worship would go on for another twenty or thirty minutes. Then the cycle would continue with more prophecies and more worship.

I was personally involved in worship services of this type in the early 1950's that lasted three or four hours. It was a new sound that had not been heard since the days of the early Church, and before that, the days of David's Tabernacle.

Psalms, Hymns and Spiritual Songs. New understanding came with regard to Paul's words in Colossians 3:16 that the saints were to be "teaching and admonishing one another with psalms, hymns and spiritual songs." The psalms were the scriptures of the book of Psalms, set to contemporary music. Hymns were the past-movement songs that had been collected in hymnals.

Spiritual songs referred to two kinds of singing: Jesus singing in the midst of His Church through the spirit of prophecy in prophetic song (He.2:12), and the saints singing their prophecies to bring edification, exhortation and comfort to the congregation (1Cor.14:1,14). The prophetic song would sometimes be an expression of love and appreciation to the Lord from the inspired spirit of the saint, such as inspired songs of David found in the book of Psalms; and sometimes it was the voice of the Lord to His Church.

This was a fulfillment of Jeremiah's prophecy concerning restoration in the last days of the Church:

> Thus saith the Lord: "Again there shall be heard in this place [the Church]...the voice of joy, and the voice of gladness, the voice of the bridegroom, and the voice of the bride, the voice of them that shall say, Praise the Lord of hosts: for the Lord is good; for his mercy endureth forever: and of them that shall bring the sacrifice of praise into the house of the Lord. For I will cause to return the captivity of the land, as at the first, saith the Lord" (Jer.33:10-11).

It was the restoration of Jesus the Bridegroom and His Church-Bride expressing their thoughts and love to each other with the voice of prophecy and spiritual song.

Praise Dancing. The Latter Rain Movement also added another dimension to worship: what they called "faith-praise-dance." This was completely different from the Pentecostal way of "dancing in the Spirit," which was normally expressed as an uncontrolled, eyes-shut, emotionally frenzied dance.

I was personally present at the Crescent Beach Bible Conference in 1954 in British Columbia, when this type of worship was birthed in the Latter Rain Movement. I described the scene briefly in *The Eternal Church*:

> The congregation of about eight hundred people had been worshipping God for quite some time. As the worship lowered to a melodious murmur, suddenly a sister began to prophesy, "The King is coming, the King is coming—go ye out to meet Him with dances and rejoicing." She started taking ferns out of the flower basket and waving them in the air and laying some of them as if before the Lord as she praised the Lord in the

dance across the auditorium in front of the platform. The head of the conference started to stop her but the Holy Spirit told him not to, for it was of God. Within a few minutes most of the audience was praising God with legs swinging and bodies moving in rhythmic praise to God.

The Scripture contains more examples of praising the Lord in the dance than it does examples of lifting hands, clapping, shouting, singing from hymnals, or many other worship practices within Christendom. King David, the man after God's own heart, praised the Lord in the dance; and the Psalms—which served as the worship book for the New Testament Church— gives several commands to praise God in the dance (Ps.149:3; 150:4; 30:11; Acts 13:22; 2Sam.6:14-16; Jer.31:4,13; Eccl.3:14; Mt.11:17; Lk.15:25).

Charismatic Worship. The Charismatic Movement incorporated all of these restored ways of worship and added Jewish-style folk dance steps as well. During this time choreographed dance and sign language hand movements were combined as well to express the words of Christian songs and to amplify the emphasis of the message visually. Women designed colorful folk costume-type dresses that thoroughly covered their bodies so that they could praise dance decently and in order. The Kingdom Movement churches and others extended praise dance to include ballet, with accompanying ballet attire.

Controversy Over Dance in Worship. Most Faith Movement leaders are direct spiritual descendants of the Pentecostal Movement and were activated into more of the supernatural ministry by the Deliverance Evangelism Movement in 1947 and 1948. They were never involved in the restoration ways of worship that the Latter Rain Movement brought into the Church.

Nevertheless, many Faith people and Word churches practiced some of these ways of worship until one of their leaders made an issue of his personal conviction about the matter. He insisted that the Pentecostal way of "dancing in the Spirit" was acceptable in the Church, but the Latter Rain and Charismatic ways of choreographed dance and "praise dancing" were not. This caused contention and division within the Church.

Nevertheless, these ways of worship were genuinely restored to the Church by the Holy Spirit, and the Holy Spirit will not be involved in any teaching that belittles or discounts anything God has restored to His Church. Each group has a right to their own convictions, but not a right to cause contention and strife by judging and condemning another group's ways of worship which are just as scriptural as theirs.

A Prophetic Movement Minstrel. The Holy Spirit has been faithful to raise up a young prophet minstrel among us. Robert Gay has been brought forth to put music to the message that some of the Prophetic Movement leaders are prophesying and teaching. God has already inspired him to write hundreds of choruses and to produce audio cassettes of prophetic worship music. We can see in Scripture where the ministry of the prophet and the minstrel were often linked together. Elijah called for a minstrel before delivering the word of the Lord (2Ki.3:15). Also we see where many of the sons of the prophets of Samuel's school of the prophets became some of the chief musicians of David's Tabernacle (1Sam.10:1-27). We can see why the restoration of David's Tabernacle and the Prophetic Movement are tied together (Acts 15:16).

Robert recounts an example of how the prophetic message can give birth to new music:

> In a service at the CI center in April 1988, Bishop Hamon brought forth a prophecy to the congregation during worship. The prophecy witnessed so strongly to my spirit that I transcribed its words and read it over many times. One phrase in the prophecy really seemed to stick with me: "I'm arising as a mighty man of war."
>
> About a month later I was at home having lunch. After I finished I got up to go back to work, but before I

walked out the door I had a vision in which I saw Jesus riding on a horse in knee-deep fog, wielding a sword with fire in His eyes. Everything seemed to be in slow motion as Jesus came closer and closer. Then the vision stopped and I heard the Spirit of God say, "Write what you see."

I opened my mouth and began to sing this song: "He's arising, arising in our midst as a mighty man of war/Clothed in battle armor and wielding a two-edged sword./We're conquering all His enemies and laying them at His feet./So arise O God, arise as a man of war, mighty man of war!" The prophetic word was the **seed** for that song, and the **vision from the Holy Spirit** activated it in my spirit, bringing forth clarity and understanding of the words and music that resulted in the song "Mighty Man of War."

Robert's choruses portray the message of the restoration of prophets. They also demonstrate the spirit of warfare praise that is the new dimension of worship being restored in this movement. The music's message is reflected in words like "God is still speaking today (by His prophets)"; "We are the Joshua generation, we are the people that will take command." The music has an intense quality that urges holiness, victorious living and all-out devotion and surrender to Jesus Christ.

Robert has written over two hundred choruses, and twenty-five of them have been professionally recorded on two cassettes produced by CI-NPM: **Prophetic Praises I** *"Mighty Man of War"*; **Prophetic Praises II** *"Roar, Lion of Judah."* He has also had 12 songs recorded on Integrity's Hosanna! Music worship tapes, 5 of which were on their last tape of the 80's, **"Victor's Crown"** for which Robert was the worship leader.

The chorus Robert felt inspired to write for our first regional prophets conference in Atlanta, Georgia, in August 1989, has the same title as the theme for our conference: **"Let Us Prepare the Way."** This chorus gives the core of the message of the prophetic:

> Let us prepare the way
> For the coming of the Lord;
> Let us prepare the way
> For the coming of our King;
> For the prophets of the Lord God
> Will arise in this hour,
> Declaring words of wisdom
> With glory and with power.
> We will see a demonstration
> As His voice is heard
> And the Glory of God will fill the earth
> As we prophesy His Word.

These praise choruses convey the words and spirit of a militant army ready to possess their promised land. The "Joshua Generation" has crossed over their spiritual Jordan restorationally. They are now marching around Jericho, preparing to fulfill their predestined purpose as one of the restorational, present-truth "tribes" that will be joined together in spirit and truth to drive out all the "ites" of Canaan.

This prophetic group, along with other groups of similar faith and vision, will go forth with the high praises of the Word of God in their mouth and the two-edged sword in their hands. They will speak the Logos and rhema word of God to execute the judgments written by all the prophets in the Scriptures. They will fulfill all the promises given to the prophet Abraham, the father of all God's prophetic people (Ps.149:6-9; Gen.20:7; Rom.4:16).

8

A CRY FOR BALANCE, STRUCTURE AND ORDER

The September 1989 issue of *Charisma* magazine featured a cover story surveying the Prophetic Movement. An accompanying editorial by the publisher, Stephen Strang, made an earnest appeal to prophetic leaders to make sure the movement is maintained with integrity and balance. He discussed some legitimate concerns about the potential for extreme teaching and practices in this movement, and I am in full agreement with his concerns. Strang said:

> If abuses begin springing up in this new prophecy movement (and sadly, we are beginning to hear of some isolated instances where this is the case), then the danger of abuse goes far beyond what we ever saw in the discipleship movement.
>
> We call on Bill Hamon, Paul Cain and some of the others emerging as leaders in this movement to see that this gift is not abused. We are happy that Hamon has, for example, instituted a policy of checking out the ministry of those submitted to him. The use of tape recordings of prophecies helps cut down on potential abuse. But even more needs to be done. There needs to be a great deal of teaching in the area.

This goal is actually my own heart's desire and determination. By the grace of God and wisdom granted, I will do all within my power and resources to maintain integrity and balance.

Understanding the Process. Nevertheless, others must understand the process that every restoration movement has gone through since the beginning of the great restoration of the Church. The leaders and people who are being used by God to restore the old biblical truth and spiritual experiences are initially rejected, persecuted and made total outcasts from the established Christian denominations and past movement groups. They become the subject of the greatest controversy within the Church; they are accused of being fanatics, heretics, false prophets or teachers—even cult leaders (Mt.23:29-39).

Only as the movement grows and gradually establishes hundreds of churches throughout the world who propagate and practice the same things will the old-order church leaders finally grant them a tolerable status, allowing them to exist without constant harassment. (The Charismatic Movement churches have only now evolved to that status). The new movement churches are then finally allowed to join the rest of the Christian community after the fire of the movement has leveled off into an organized structure and some kind of predictable performance.

Hot War and Cold War. Thus a divine restoration of truth first brings about a "hot war" between those who accept it and those who reject it. After the battle is over and almost everyone has either stayed with the old or gone with the new, the two groups evolve into a "cold war" relationship, practicing mutual tolerance without fully accepting one another as fellow members of the Body of Christ worthy of their love and fellowship.

Extreme Swings in the Pendulum of Restored Truth. When truth is in the process of being restored to the Church, it usually swings extremely to the right, then to the left, and finally hangs straight with a balanced message, like the pendulum of a grandfather clock, in the middle of the two extremes. Those who get stuck out on the extreme left become cultic in their doctrines and practices. Those who don't make it back from the extreme right become an exclusive group who separate themselves from the rest of the Body of Christ. Then there is the group who brings itself together from both extremes to maintain a balance in proper biblical doctrine and practice as God originally intended it to be restored within the Church.

A restoration movement may also be compared to the times when a heavy rain comes and causes a river to flood over its banks. Some of the water gets stuck out on the right side of the river and forms little ponds where a few fish stay. Some of the water on the left never makes it back to the river but forms bayous and swamps where all kinds of slimy and poisonous creatures dwell. As the flood waters recede the main body of water flows between the river banks of wisdom and maturity in ministering the restored truths and spiritual experiences.

The "Balanced" Group May Lose the Anointing. Nevertheless, the "balanced" group may become so protective of the truth and so reactionary toward the extremists that they keep the original form yet lose the flow of the Holy Spirit. They may keep the purity of the doctrine yet lose the fresh anointing that restored those truths. They may maintain the proper preaching and practices yet lose God's mighty presence and power that originally accompanied their ministry.

Sad to say, Church history reveals that it is this balanced group that usually becomes the main persecutors of the next restorational movement of the Holy Spirit. They establish wineskins of doctrinal limitations with regard to what, when, where, who and how the truth can be ministered. Their wineskins become dry and set with such limitations that they cannot receive the new wine of restored truth that adds new truth and spiritual ministries to the Church.

Be Established in the Present Truth. For that reason, we must keep our wineskins flexible so that we can go from movement to movement of the Holy Spirit, incorporating into our personal lives and our churches all that God wants to restore to His Church (2Cor.3:18). At the same time, we must not become vulnerable to extremism and fanaticism. As the Apostle Peter declared, we must continually "be established in the present truth" without forsaking any of the truths and practices which have already been restored (2Pet.1:12). Jesus said that a wise scribe is one who brings out of his treasure chest treasure both old and new. The Church is not a water tank or salty dead sea, but a river of fresh-flowing, life-giving water (Mt.13:52; Ez. 47:1-12; Jn.7:38).

Abuses Cannot Be Totally Prevented. The true apostles and prophets who are called to pioneer this Prophetic Movement will do all they can to maintain balance and to keep prophetic ministers from doing foolish things that bring disgrace and reproach upon the movement. But none of the past restoration movements were able to prevent abuses and extremes totally, and neither will we be able to do so.

The fact remains that there will always be those who are biblically uneducated and who never become birthed in the present truth. There will always be those who are emotionally unstable and spiritually immature who cannot handle the truth, so they start doing weird things that are out of order concerning the present truth. And there will always be charlatans, false ministers and those who are wrongly motivated, looking for an opportunity to promote themselves and to profit from the movement.

These three groups could be called the fanatical right, the extreme left and the middle hangers, balanced between the two extremes. A brief resume of the major truths restored over the last five centuries will reveal that every movement has had these three groups.

The 1500's—Justification by Faith. This pendulum of truth swung from the one extreme of salvation by works with no faith, to the other extreme of all faith and no works of righteousness with their faith. Those who walked on in the truth came to a balance in the middle. They were justified by faith, demonstrating their faith by works of obedience to righteous living. There were also the theological extremes of Calvinism and Armenianism, along with those who took a balanced position between the two extremes.

The 1600's—Water Baptism. There were the two extremes of those who preached that a person was not saved until he or she was water-baptized by immersion versus those who put little value on water baptism. There were those who taught that a baby could receive all the blessings of Christianity through water baptism and there were those who taught that a child could receive nothing from the Lord until the age of twelve. Those who walked on in truth developed a balance between these extremes.

The 1700's—Holiness, Sanctification and Perfectionism. With regard to holiness teaching, there were the two extremes of legalism and liberty. The legalist believed all sports, amusements and current fashions were sinful for Christians. The liberty extremists declared that grace gave license for all things, proclaiming that "to the pure all things are pure."

With regard to teaching on sanctification, one extreme insisted that Christians have only one eternally sanctifying experience, while the other extreme said we need to be sanctified daily. Perfectionism had its two extremes of those who made no allowance for a Christian ever sinning, and those who believed a Christian cannot avoid sinning a little every day.

Thank God there is a balance between these extremes of a divine truth. Those who pressed on in present truth maintained a balance between these extreme positions in the teachings and practices of the restored truth.

The 1800's—The Second Coming of Jesus. There were the two extremes of those who proclaimed Christ's imminent return and set dates for His coming, using every world event and calamity as proof, and those who did not believe in a literal return of Christ at all. The great theological controversies were over eschatological viewpoints: premillennialism, postmillennialism and amillennialism. Those who were premillennialist went to extremes in their eschatological preaching about whether there would be a pretribulation, midtribulation, or posttribulation rapture of the Church.

The 1880's—Divine Faith Healing. The theological controversy was whether the stripes Jesus received provided healing for the physical body just as His death on the cross provided forgiveness of sins. In other words, was there physical healing in the atonement of Christ Jesus?

Those who did accept the teaching of healing in the atonement developed different extreme beliefs: Some believed that divine faith was the only acceptable remedy for the physical healing of Christians (with the use of medical care forbidden); those on the opposite side exhausted all natural means before turning to Jesus for supernatural divine healing. Those who maintained the restoration truth of divine healing did so with a balance between those extreme swings to the right and to the left.

The 1900's—Holy Ghost Baptism and Other Tongues. The theological problem was whether the "unknown tongue" is the only valid scriptural evidence of having received the gift of the Holy Ghost. Among the Pentecostals who accepted tongues-talking there were two extreme groups: those who believed a person was not saved until he or she spoke in tongues, and those who believed there were several different divine proofs (such as the Holiness Movement proclaimed) of the baptism of the Holy Ghost.

The Pentecostals also went to extremes in concepts of the Godhead, with some teaching a form of unitarianism (the doctrine that there is no Trinity—known as the "Jesus Only" doctrine) and some, tritheism (the doctrine that denies the unity of the three Persons of the Godhead). These groups also developed hard religious attitudes concerning water baptism formulas.

There were differences of opinion concerning the proper terminology for describing this "other tongues" experience. Some called it "Spirit-baptized" and some, "Spirit-filled." Some argued over whether we should say it is the baptism with, in, into, by, or of the Holy Ghost.

The terminology used did not hinder the Holy Ghost from baptizing believers. But some groups went into such fanaticism that they eventually destroyed themselves. Others segregated themselves from the rest of the Body of Christ by declaring that all church groups were wrong except themselves. They felt they were the only Pentecostal group who had true salvation and the proper teaching and ministries of the restored truth.

Consequently, scores of Pentecostal denominations and independent groups were established. Most of them still do not grant each other the right hand of fellowship. But there were some major Pentecostal denominations who maintained the original form, doctrines and spiritual ministries of the truth that the Holy Spirit wanted to restore at that time.

The 1940's—Laying on of Hands and Personal Prophecy. The controversial truth being restored was what has come to be known as 'prophetic presbytery'. The issue was whether or not Holy Spirit-filled ministers had the biblical right and spiritual power to prophetically reveal to ministers their fivefold ascension gift calling and to prophesy to saints their membership ministry within the Body of Christ. Also they taught that by prophecy and the laying on of hands Holy Spirit gifts could be revealed and activated within saints (1Tim.4:14; 1:18).

This pendulum of truth had its far swings to the right and left before becoming balanced in the middle. Some Latter Rain Ministers relegated prophecy to certain appointed apostles and prophets. Others allowed anyone, at any time, without proper supervision, to prophesy to anyone else.

As in every movement, those who maintained the truth in balance established guidelines for teaching and ministering the truth restored. The extremist groups have self-destructed and the pressing-on, balanced groups have preserved the truth in the purity of preaching and practice.

The 1950's—Praise-Singing, Body Ministry, Praise-Dancing. The difference in scriptural emphasis was between those who believed saints could melodiously sing praises and those who thought praise should only be with the Pentecostal shout. Others debated whether spiritual ministry should be released among the body of believers in the congregation or be totally directed and ministered from the pulpit.

In one extreme, whole church services were given to praise and prophecies with very little value put on preaching, while many others continued to view worship only as a preliminary to the total pre-eminence of the preaching of the Word. Another extreme group established what they called the heavenly hierarchy of twelve apostles and twenty-four elders. They dressed themselves in religious attire like the Old Testament high priests.

Some churches had only slow melodious worship, while others had praise with dancing and shouting for hours. Some argued over whether "dancing before the Lord" was a willful act of faith in praise expression or an uncontrollable "dancing in the Spirit." There were those who believed that church services were mainly for worship and perfecting each other in Christ while others believed the whole role of the Church was to evangelize the world.

Those who walked on in the restored truth and ministries on all these issues brought a balance between the extremes and maintained the truth in purity of practice.

The 1960's—Demonology: Oppression, Obsession, or Possession? The "unknown tongues" issue had been a controversy within the Church since the Pentecostal movement so it was not a new issue to them in the 1960's. But some of the Charismatic Movement leaders caused a further controversy to arise concerning the activity of demons. This issue was whether a born-again, Holy Spirit-baptized Christian could have demon activity within his or her life to the extent that the demons needed to be cast out.

The controversy developed between those who taught that every negative thought, action and physical affliction was a demon which had to be exorcised before the Christian could change or be healed, and those who believed that the blood of

Jesus gave immunity to all who had been cleansed from their sins, because the demons could not "cross the blood line." By the mid-1970's most Charismatics had developed a balanced doctrine and practice concerning demonology.

The 1970's—Discipleship, Family Life, Church Growth and Structure. The Holy Spirit was preparing the Church for great numerical growth in the 1970's. Many churches in South America and Korea especially developed the concept of one large church congregation with numerous cell groups meeting in homes of the church members. The Holy Spirit was seeking to bring mutual respect among the ministers and willing recognition and submission to each other.

Theocratic government was being restored in the Church and the family with the proper chain of command. There was a restoration for proper order of personal priorities, especially for those in leadership and ministry: God first, wife and family second, then ministry.

However, the inevitable extremes appeared. Some taught and developed a Christian leadership pyramid. The pastor became almost a papal leader to those under him. All single adult women had to have a male "covering" to be in divine order. All decisions had to be made by leadership, even daily and personal activities of members. Leaders became domineering and made those under them totally dependent on them.

Some groups went to the other extremes of doing away with church leadership structure by changing from pastorship to co-eldership. Some disbanded the weekly united meeting of a large congregation, breaking it up into small house meeting cell groups only. Some did away with the Sunday night service to make it a home family night.

A "Jesus Movement" came out of the worldly young peoples' rebellion against society (the hippie movement). They were more inclined to be opposed to church structure. Nevertheless, they helped deliver the Church from some of its ritualistic traditions. By the end of the decade most non-denominational present-truth Charismatic churches had developed a balance in doctrine and practice concerning discipleship, shepherding, family life and Church structure.

When there is a flooding of truth and ministry, the river of the Church overflows its banks. Some water does not make it back into the mainstream, but becomes ponds and bayous. Thus some extreme left and right groups became bayous while God's restoring Church settled into the banks of the river and flowed on in order and balance.

The 1970's—Faith Message, Prosperity, Word Teaching. For centuries the Church had taught that spirituality and poverty were synonymous. The practice of monasticism and asceticism that developed during the Dark Ages was still influencing the Church. Those from the Holiness, Pentecostal and Latter Rain Movements were still under the impression that it was worldly and carnal to have wealth or modern conveniences, or to wear and drive the latest and best.

Oral Roberts was one of the first to propagate the idea that God is a good God and desires Christians to be in health and to prosper, even as their soul prospers (3Jn. 1:2). But it was not until the 1970's that the truth started being practiced enough to become a worldwide controversy.

Three Camps. The teaching of victorious, prosperous, healthy living in the natural and spiritual came from three different camps: (1) Oral Roberts's ministry of teaching the seed faith principle of sowing and reaping, of sowing finances to reap finances; (2) Robert Schueller's ministry of positive living and success principles; (3) the group of ministers who became known as "prosperity preachers," "the Faith message teachers," or the "Word People." A few of the well-known leaders were Kenneth Hagin, Kenneth Copeland, Hobart Freeman and Fred Price.

The Holy Spirit was striving to bring the Body of Christ to a new faith level and a greater revelation of truth so that the material things needed could be brought in to communicate the gospel and prosper the Church. Nevertheless, as in the activation and restoration of every truth, different groups became "stuck" on the extreme swings of the pendulum of truth restoration.

The Extremes. Some of the groups that developed in this movement taught and cultivated the attitude that any Christian who was not wealthy and healthy was either an unbeliever or out of fellowship with God. They taught that God does not try the righteous. If you did not have a miracle every day and prosperity all the way, you were not a faith person.

Others became selfish and mammon-motivated ministers who took the truth about prosperity and turned it into an opportunity to take inordinate offerings for themselves. Some tried to use the teaching as the basis for get-rich schemes that ended in bankruptcy—hurting many people along the way.

Still others went to extremes on confession and positive declarations until their teaching approximated the doctrines of Christian Science. Still others swung to the opposite side, declaring that believers have no control over their lives; that they must simply accept whatever comes their way as the will of God; that poverty and sickness are used by God to perfect the saints; and that sickness and poverty must therefore be suffered gracefully. Thank God there is a balance between these extremes.

The old controversy that arose during the Divine Healing Movement of the 1880's arose again among the Faith people. Anyone who used medicine, consulted a physician, or had surgery was looked down upon by one group of extremists.

Regardless of the differences in the various camps, these ministers were instrumental in establishing the Church on the biblical principles of overcoming faith, prosperity, faith healing, the power of the Word and the necessity of a continual positive confession. They wrote hundreds of books and made thousands of audio cassette tapes giving scriptural principles for prosperity, health and happiness. By the mid-1980's the movement had fulfilled its restoration mission, and those who had avoided the extremes were pressing on in the restoration truth and ministry.

The 1980's—Kingdom Now, Dominion Theology, Reconstructionism. The Holy Spirit wanted to bring the Church to a dominion attitude and to become more concerned about God's kingdom coming than the Church leaving. He wanted the Church to come out from under its bushel and let its light shine upon the whole world and not just in the Church.

God desires to demonstrate to the world that His Church really is the salt of the earth, and that Christians should be involved in every legitimate activity of humankind to be a witness and influence for the kingdom of God. Separation of church and state does not mean the separation of Christians from the roles of lawyers, senators, corporate managers and even President of the United States.

Controversy Over the Kingdom. The Kingdom message emphasized the biblical truth that the saints have been made kings and priests to God and shall rule and reign on the earth. The great controversy was over who, when, where and how God's literal kingdom will be established over planet earth. The basic conflict came between reformed theology and evangelical theology, and the different views of pre-, post-, and amillennialists concerning the timing and strategy of the establishment of God's kingdom on earth as it is in heaven.

The teaching that acted as a catalyst to make the issue become a controversy within the Church was that of Bishop Earl Paulk of Chapel Hill Harvester Church in Atlanta. His emphasis was on a view of the rapture which to most Evangelicals and Pentecostals was a denial of the rapture bordering on heresy. He taught that the departed saints would be resurrected and the living saints would be translated in the twinkling of an eye, but this was not for the purpose of leaving the earth. Rather, it was for establishing God's divine order for the human race and Christ's rulership over all the earth.

Some Extremes. As with every movement, different groups arose that laid hold of what God was trying to do and took it to extremes: Some propagated a Christian revolutionary political takeover by natural means without operating in the supernatural power of God. Others pulled back and said that there is nothing the Church can do but pray and hope for the best while the world gets worse and Jesus finally returns to take the Church off to heaven.

Some went into choreographed dancing in ballet fashion to express the music and words to Christian songs. Others went to the extreme of declaring that any worship that was planned and practiced for presentation was unscriptural, and that only the old Pentecostal "dancing in the Spirit" was acceptable to God.

By the end of the 1980's those who propagated the Kingdom message had come to a basic biblical position that the Church is a kingdom witness to all society and that we must demonstrate the kingdom not only in practical ways but also by the supernatural power of God.

The 1980's and 90's—Prophets, the Prophetic Movement, a Prophetic People. This brings us to the current wave of the restoration of truth. The Prophetic Movement is the cutting edge move of the Holy Spirit. It is restorationally activating into workable reality vital biblical truths and ministries within the twentieth-century Church of Jesus Christ.

Like every other movement, the Prophetic Movement will have those among it who will take it to the extremes of right and left. Some prophetic ministers will be unethical and wrongly motivated, attempting to use prophecy to manipulate others for their own purposes. These will fall and pass away, but in the process they will bring reproach upon the truth and will hurt others. But thanks be to God, there will nevertheless be those true prophetic ministers who will establish and maintain a proper balance in the middle.

Abuses and Extremes in the Use Of Personal Prophecy. As with every move of God, the prophetic movement will produce its share of abuses in the sense of people carrying it too far or totally misapplying the truths God is restoring. God's Spirit is pure and restores unadulterated truth and ministry, but unfortunately it is poured into earthen vessels which can be faulty (2Cor.4:7).

We have seen some abuses on a small scale already, and I want to raise a warning against perverting or using the truths being restored for personal gain or for other ungodly purposes. Specific things that we as honest Christians can make sure we avoid are these:

An Overemphasis on Personal Prophecy. Some Christians will think they need a "word from the Lord" to make every major and minor decision. They will no longer depend on their personal convictions and the Holy Spirit leadings (or pastoral counsel and wisdom) to walk daily before the Lord. In some lives personal prophecy will replace personal prayer and hearing from God for oneself.

This is not of the Lord. Personal prophecy has a valid place in the Church and the lives of individual Christians, but it was never intended to be a "quick fix" or replacement for seeking God.

Another form this abuse will take is an elevation of prophecy to the same level of authority and inspiration as the written Word of God, causing cultic groups who esteem prophetic utterance as Scripture. However, all orthodox Christians believe that the Scriptures are complete and sufficient, and will reject all extra-biblical revelation claiming authority equal to the Bible.

Ministering Out from under Authority. Some Christians will begin to prophesy in places other than those the leadership has sanctioned as appropriate. At our seminars we call these "parking lot prophecies," in which people draw others outside of meetings and prophesy strange things to them. We have a list of guidelines we've developed which we require our local church and seminar attendees to read and abide by.

We believe it is vitally important that all prophecies be given only under spiritual oversight, and also that they be tape-recorded. This allows the local eldership to adjust or correct any words which are false, wrongly applied or untimely, saving the person who is receiving the prophecy from confusion or misunderstanding. However, some who are new to this movement will prophesy helter-skelter as they are "led of the spirit?" without allowing their words to be weighed and evaluated (1Cor. 14:31; 1Thess.5:21). The prophetic ministry has the power to either bless or curse, so all words must be witnessed to and judged by those who are spiritually mature and are in oversight in the local assembly.

Using Prophecy to Justify Rebellion and Sin. The Charismatic Movement caused many prayer groups and unstructured meetings to break themselves off from the Church. Some were of God, as the Holy Spirit poured out new wine which old wineskins couldn't contain, causing inevitable splits. However, many others were just rebellious groups who wanted to do their own thing without any oversight.

The Prophetic Movement will see a continuation of this trend, with personal prophecy used as a tool to justify rebellious factions and groups. When confronted by spiritual authority they will say "God told me," and will produce as evidence several prophecies they gave themselves or others gave them which endorse their group or ministry. God never intended prophecy to judge doctrinal or disciplinary matters, and He certainly has not appointed certain saints in the Church to straighten everybody else out through their spiritual ministry.

Controlling or Manipulating Others through Prophetic Ministry. Some ministers or leaders who already have a problem with being controlling will use the gift of prophecy to dictate "orders from God" to those under them. The abuses of the discipleship movement may pale in comparison to this type of abuse of personal prophecy. Ministers will prophesy to people about whom to marry, which job to get, and when and where to move, all in the name of "spiritual revelation."

Scores of ignorant and immature saints will follow their spiritual leaders because they seem to prophesy the word of the

Lord and have signs following their ministry. So Christians must understand the difference between obeying the word of the Lord and getting confirmations on major moves and life's decisions. Study Deut.13:1-5 to understand the reasons why God allows things like this to take place.

Using the Prophetic Gifting for Personal Gain. This abuse will take two forms of deceit as certain ministers see people flocking to the prophetic because God's anointing is upon it. Many will begin to hold "prophetic conferences" which are prophetic in name only. They will be more interested in drawing people in to pay large seminar fees to bolster the finances of their church than to minister prophetically to the people.

We will begin to hear the word "prophetic" hung like a tag on nearly everything in the Church to try to carnally manipulate people to come be a part of ministries which are not at all prophetic. The second form of this abuse is as ancient as Balaam, who tried to prophesy for his own personal gain. Even now certain ones prophesy, "Thus saith the Lord, God is saying if you will support His servant with a one-time gift of $1,000 He will surely bless you."

Thousands of gullible Christians will send their money, thinking the man is speaking for God. In the end, however, these false prophets will be exposed as charlatans and judged for making merchandise of the gift of God.

Trying to Fulfill Personal Prophecy Out of Proper Timing. Many Christians who receive true personal prophecies about some great ministry or life situation will misunderstand God's dealing over a period of time and run out to try to fulfill their prophecy in their own strength. If God tells them prophetically they are going to be raised up as a great pastor, prophet, or apostle, they will run out and print business cards with titles and proclaim themselves as God's wonder-worker.

Others who are called to be financial stewards for the kingdom of God will rush into business situations based on a personal prophesy because they think one prophecy will cause them to prosper in all their endeavors. The results will be broken contracts, bankruptcy and ruined lives. When a true prophecy is spoken to an individual, God intends to accomplish that prophecy at some point in that person's life, not necessarily in the next week or month. Christians will have to learn to wait on the timing of the Lord. (Please see chapters 16 and 17 in *Prophets and Personal Prophecy* to determine the proper response to a personal prophecy, and chapter 10 to learn about "Personal Prophecy and Business Endeavors.")

Presumptuous, Critical and Judgmental Prophesying. One of the greatest dangers and abuses to the Prophetic Movement will be people prophesying presumptuously or critically. For some reason, folks with a critical and negative spirit seem to flock to prophetic ministry, feeling that congregational or personal prophecy is their platform to blast everyone else for living in sin (and indirectly implying that they themselves are the true standard for righteousness). I've seen and heard many who felt they were God's lone prophet in the wilderness proclaiming righteousness while the rest of the Church was wicked and sinful (Deut. 18:20-22).

I've found, however, that the result of such prophesying is bitter, fruitless and condemning. God has not anointed any sheriffs in the kingdom of God to judge and condemn others, and I found He will rarely, if ever, use immature saints and ministers to give a true word of rebuke and correction. This will be instead left to the mature person whom God can trust with hard words that need to be delivered in the spirit of humility and healing.

These are just a few of the areas that can move out of balance in prophetic ministry. I plan to cover many more of them in the next book of this series.

Not Just a Fad. The Prophetic Movement contains vital truths and ministries that Christ wants established within His Church. It is not a religious fad or just a temporary renewal of a previously restored truth or ministry. *The restoration of prophets and the*

prophetic ministry is absolutely essential for the fulfillment of
Christ's progressive purpose for His Church and His ultimate
purpose for planet earth.

The decade of the 1980's was the season for the conception,
development and birthing of the Prophetic Movement. This last
decade of the twentieth century will be used to spread it to the
ends of the world and to establish the truth and ministries the
Holy Spirit was commissioned to restore in this movement.

The Restoration Cycle of History. Every true restoration movement has gone through the same historic process and cycle:
First, the truth is injected into the heart of key ministers God
plans to use. Then in His timing it is projected into the Church.

Initially it is rejected by the majority of church leaders. This
causes much persecution for a period of time until the movement
has ministers and churches established around the world. Then
they are passively endured for years until they are finally considered biblical enough to be accepted into the Christian community of churches which are no longer branded a cult.

Rejection and Persecution Ahead. The Prophetic Movement
has gone through the stages of injection and projection, and is
now receiving enough prominence to receive rejection and
persecution. Those ministers and churches who propagate the
prophetic will continue on until the rest of the Church world
either passively endures them or accepts them. Those who
accept and believe that this is something that Christ wants
established in His corporate Body will allow the truths and
ministries to be incorporated into their teachings, practices and
ways of worship.

Our enemy, the devil, hates God's prophets and the prophetic ministry. He is bringing forth whatever will help bring
rejection and persecution. Already, as in other movements, the
charlatans, novices, ignorant, immature and wrongly motivated
people who are normally on the outer fringes and not in the
main flow are beginning to use the product of the prophetic
improperly for their own profit.

Such wrongly motivated actions and presumptuous prophesying will cause those church leaders with righteous integrity and moral biblical standards to reject such religious nonsense. But this is not the true "baby" movement; it is the dirty "bath water"—and we must not throw the baby out with the bath water. The "fathers" who were used to birth the movement have the true spirit and purpose of the movement and are normally not the ones who make merchandise of the restorational truths and ministries.

Abuses Have Already Begun. It greatly grieves my spirit, saddens my heart and even at times stirs a righteous indignation in me when I see and hear how some are already using and abusing the truths and ministries of the prophetic. Even now, there are those with television programs who are using the ministry of prophesying to manipulate people to give them financial support. They close their eyes and point their finger and say, "The Lord says and the Lord shows me" that someone is to send them a certain amount of money. If the Lord ever did anoint them to prophesy, then that anointing left when they started using the gift for personal promotion and manipulating for money.

I was shocked and disgusted when I heard another television personality say, "Write to me and I will send you your personal prophecy tape for personal prosperity." I sent for it so I could hear for myself what was said. It was a soulish sham of using the prophetic to manipulate and motivate people to support his ministry.

"There Must Also Be Heresies." I sometimes wish I had the power to cut them off and close their mouths, but then the Lord reminds me of what Paul told the Corinthian church. He said, "For there must be also heresies among you, that they who are approved may be made manifest among you" (1Cor.11:19). In relation to this movement that means that there must be the false prophets, the ignorant, the immature and the wrongly motivated prophetic ministers who are improperly using the office of prophet and the ministry of prophesying, so that those who are true and proper may be made manifest as the true prophets within Christ's Church. Jesus said for us to let the tares grow along with the wheat until the time of harvest (Mt. 13:24-30).

Please understand that all the truly God-ordained fathers within the prophetic movement will be doing all in their power to teach, write books and produce teaching manuals giving biblical guidelines as fast as they can, for the proper administration of these truths and ministries. The ideal is to keep proper structure, order and practice while the truths and ministries are being restored with nothing ever done to bring reproach upon the ministry. That is the **ideal** that a few will fulfill, but the **real** is that it has never worked that way totally in any movement.

Let All Things Be Done. Paul declared, "Let all things be done decently and in order" (1Cor.14:40). But there is no need for decency and order unless something is being done. The emphasis should be put upon the first five words in the statement as much as it is on the last four: **Let all things be done!** The preacher of old declared that the only way to have a clean stall was to not have an ox in it (Prov.14:4).

In the beginning of a movement, all the teaching done at seminars and the books written major on proclaiming what God is restorationally doing. The preaching that goes forth is that 'because it is of God, we should "let all things be done".' Then, after the movement has gone through projection, rejection, persecution and passivity, most of the books written deal with balance, proper procedures and how to be more compatible and acceptable to the rest of the church world. At that time the last half of that statement is focused upon, everything in the movement is done "decently and in order."

The ones who do not manifest the truth as God intended are the ones who do not make it back to the middle from the extreme swings of the pendulum of restored truth. Those who have the heart of God and mind of Christ for this movement will proceed on with proper prophetic procedures and practices.

9

THE SPIRIT OF TRUE PROPHETS
AND
THE PROPHETIC MOVEMENT

I want to share with you what I believe must be the spirit of all true prophets of God and those who participate in the Prophetic Movement. Being a true prophet entails much more than speaking a true word or having a miracle ministry. In fact, it is possible for a true prophet to speak an incorrect word, since all human beings are fallible and prone to make mistakes.

Many claim that the law of Moses must still be in effect in regard to prophets, and they require prophets to be one hundred percent accurate or else be stoned (blackballed in ministry). However, we see that the other offenses worthy of death in the Old Testament are no longer in force either. Jesus, according to the law, should have stoned the woman brought to him caught in adultery. Yet he told her "go and sin no more."

Motivation as Important as Ministry. There is much more to being a true prophet than just the words spoken or miracles worked. Even a prophetic minister who is unrighteous or immoral in some of his or her ways can actually give accurate, specific words—yet nevertheless remain in the eyes of God as a false prophet. We see this specifically in the case of Balaam, who gave the only Messianic prophecy in the book of Numbers and seemed to have a valid prophetic ministry, even though all New Testament references condemn him as a false prophet (2Pet.2:15; Jude 11). Balaam type prophets who can prophesy accurately and manifest mighty miracles, but minister without

143

the spirit of wisdom or divine love, may well hear Jesus' pronouncement concerning false prophets in Matthew 7:15-23.

Our preaching is to be doctrinally sound and our prophesying is to be accurate and bring anointed results. But many ministers can preach and prophesy accurately. God wants all of us to be known by a motivating spirit of wisdom and love. Jesus said that we would know false prophets by their fruit (of the Holy Spirit) more than by their spiritual manifestations and miracles (Mt. 7:15,16).

Body No Better than its Spirit. Every living organism has its own unique characteristics by which it is known and identified. Every human body has it own personality and spirit. The corporate Body of Christ has its own personality and spirit which is the character of Christ and the Holy Spirit of God.

Everything God creates has not only a purpose but also a motivation. Proper performance of the body is always determined by the spirit that motivates it. As founder and Bishop of the Christian International Network of Prophetic Ministries, I have received from God a commission, vision and conviction concerning the right spirit and motivation for the CI-NPM. The Holy Spirit is the overall coordinating spirit and motivating factor of all works that God has ordained. But the specific Holy Spirit motivation that God wants for the company of prophets is the **"spirit of wisdom"** (Ja.3:17) and **"faith which works by love"** (Gal.5:6; 1Cor.13:1-8).

The Spirit of Wisdom. In Ephesians 1:16-23 Paul prayed a long prayer for the Ephesian Christians. He began his prayer with this request: "that the God of our Lord Jesus Christ, the Father of glory, may give unto you the spirit of wisdom and revelation in the knowledge of Christ Jesus." Paul's first concern and desire for them was that they receive the spirit of wisdom.

Solomon says wisdom is the principal thing (Pr.4:7). But here Paul is not speaking of the intellectual understanding that wisdom brings; he means rather the **spirit of wisdom**—the attributes of wisdom used in performing its great insights. He emphasizes that the spirit of wisdom is an absolute must in a person's life before he or she can properly move into and minister supernatural "revelation." **Revelation without wisdom becomes radical and self-exalting.** Divine revelation and great prophetic insights will not be presented in proper divine order without the spirit of wisdom providing the very nature and controlling characteristics of the person prophesying.

Joshua Generation Arising. God is raising up a Joshua generation in this day and hour. Before Joshua was ready to take God's people into the promised land, Moses laid his hands upon Joshua and imparted the "spirit of wisdom" (Deut.34:9). Joshua had allowed all the characteristics of wisdom to be worked into his very nature and way of life.

Today a new generation of prophets and prophetic people is being raised up to go into God's promised land and drive out the false representations of supernatural communication—the modern equivalent of the ancient "ites" of Canaan. True prophets of God will speak more supernatural knowledge from heaven by the Holy Spirit than the occultists do from human psychic and evil spirits. The prophetic Joshua generation will be known and distinguished not only by their supernatural knowledge of people and affairs but by their spirit of wisdom. Those who do not develop the attributes and characteristics of the spirit of wisdom will be left in the wilderness to wander around, while those with Christlike attributes of the spirit of wisdom will go in to possess their promised possessions.

Wisdom's Character and Spirit. James 3:17 gives a detailed description of wisdom's spirit. Jesus is wisdom (1Cor.1:30), and His Spirit is holy so the spirit of wisdom would be the fruits of Christ's Holy Spirit. James 3:13-17 should be read in several translations to gain the full impact of what the inspired writer is saying.

Verse 13 declares that our speaking and ministering should be done **"with the meekness of wisdom."** Then in verses 17 and 18, James describes the spirit attributes of divine wisdom: *"It is*

first pure, then peaceable, gentle, and easy to be entreated, full of
mercy and good fruits, without partiality, and without hypocrisy.
And the fruit of righteousness is sown in peace of them that make
peace."

The first characteristic of the spirit of wisdom is to be **pure**.
Literally this means to be free from anything that adulterates,
taints or impairs. Something pure is unmixed and clear, like
pure water. It is free from sin or guilt; it is blameless, virgin or
chaste.

Jesus said, "Blessed are the pure in heart, for they shall see
God." (Mt.5:8) If prophets want to see God and prophetic
ministers want to move in power, they must get this purity of
heart first. It is impossible to present a pure word of the Lord if
you are not pure in heart, motive and attitude (Mt.12:33,34;
Ja.3:11).

We are living in the days of Malachi 3:3: *"And he shall sit as*
a refiner and purifier of silver: and he shall purify the sons of Levi,
and purge them as gold and silver, that they may offer unto the
Lord an offering in righteousness." God will no longer put up
with the defilement and filth that has infiltrated ministers who
are like Eli's corrupt sons—both killed in one day for their sin
before God. God is raising up some Samuels who will be
dedicated to God in purity and righteousness (1Sam.2:12-3:21).

Peaceable Prophets. The dictionary definition of **peaceable** is
"having an undisturbed state of mind, absent of mental conflict;
free from war, living in harmony, having a disposition toward
peace, not quarrelsome." Does our life exemplify this attribute
of the spirit of wisdom?

Prophets and saints operating in the spirit of wisdom are
peaceable. "Blessed are the peacemakers, for they shall be
called the children of God"(Mt.5:9). True saints and prophetic
ministers are peacemakers among different camps of belief in
the Church, and are not those who stir up strife, debate, accusa-
tions and condemnation causing war between Christian camps.
If you want to check someone out who is operating in prophetic
ministry to see if that person operates in the spirit of wisdom,

just cross him or her and see what kind of spirit is manifested when you do.

Grace of Gentleness. Gentle speaks of all that is entailed in being a gentleman, especially the old concept of an English gentleman: "One of the upper classes, of good birth, having qualities considered appropriate to those of good birth, refined, polite, noble and a gentle knight, generous, kind, easily handled, tame as a gentle dog." Like a collie, he does not bite when you touch him; you can trust him around the children. A gentle person is not violent, harsh, rude, or ill-mannered in attitude, word or actions.

The spirit of wisdom is gentle and personifies the characteristics of a gentleman. First of all, a gentleman is one born of high social standing and royalty. We are born of God, the King of the universe. We are born into the family of God Almighty. You cannot be born into any higher social order than that! In fact, we are royalty, even kings and priests unto God. Of all people on the face of the earth, prophets and saintly prophetic people should live and minister like royal gentlemen (Rev.1:6; 1Jn.1:3; 3:1-3).

Mildness implies a temper by nature which is not easily provoked. Meek is a spirit which has been schooled to mildness by discipline or suffering. These attributes are a must if we are properly to represent Jesus Christ, the prophet. Basically, a true prophet's attitude should be the Beatitudes of Christ (Mt.5:3-12).

The World's View of a Prophet. Today's prophets and prophetic ministers have the calling, privilege and responsibility to change the world's view, and most church peoples' view, of a prophet. What type of person do most people visualize when they think of a prophet? They have been conditioned to think of a wild-eyed, bushy-bearded man, ranting and raving like a maniac while crying out "Repent! For the wrath of God is upon you filthy sinners!"

This stereotypical prophet has honey matted in his beard and dripping off his chin while roasted locust legs are hanging out of his mouth. He portrays a God who is angry at the world, and he himself seems to be just as angry as his God. He has hatred and judgment for the whole world. He is rude, obnoxious, brutish, ungentlemanlike, a radical human being who lives like a hermit in a cave that is his own little world. He is unsociable, a law unto himself, and is accountable to God and no one else—only God can tell him what to do.

This is completely opposite to how the New Testament describes a person who represents Jesus Christ and is called to speak for Him. A New Testament prophet is an extension of Jesus Christ, the Prophet, and should exemplify His wisdom and personality traits, which are the fruits of the Holy Spirit. All prophets and prophetesses should be the role model of a gentleman and a lady.

Prophets are Real People. If you are **"easy to be entreated"** then you are a down-to-earth, practical, real person. You are approachable, teachable, considerate, responsive to an earnest request, with no airs that say "I am too holy and heavenly to be approached by common saints, such a holy prophet that I cannot be touched by others."

Have you ever been around certain preachers who portray the attitude that they are so holy, anointed and separated unto God that they are unapproachable? Jesus the prophet was never unapproachable.

His disciples tried to make him that way, but Jesus drew the children to himself and sat them on his lap when the disciples tried to keep them away from Him. He received the blind man that was persistently screaming out for Jesus to heal him. The disciples were trying to tell the man to be quiet and not to bother the Master Prophet, for He had more important things to do. But Jesus touched and healed the unclean leper from whom the disciples were trying to protect Him. True prophets can destroy themselves if they allow their disciples to become too overly protective of them.

True Prophets are Not Seclusive. Successful ministers who are in great demand can easily develop a life of exclusiveness and seclusion from the Church world of God's people. My joy and delight is to minister to God's people. I would say that one of the compliments my wife and I appreciate the most is when people say, "We appreciate you because you are so approachable, so down-to-earth and real." The spirit of the prophets and prophetic people should not be exclusive, seclusive or 'spooky spiritual'. They must be genuine men and women who are anointed to be God's prophets, prophetesses, prophetic ministers and prophetic people.

Men and Women of Mercy. Other attributes of the spirit of wisdom include **mercy**, which can be defined as refraining from harming or punishing offenders. It is kindness in excess of what may be expected or demanded by fairness; going the second mile, forbearance, compassion. The spirit of wisdom is full of mercy, and this is such an important characteristic for God to develop in the prophet (Ja.2:13).

　　Without mercy the prophet becomes hard, sneering, eager to prophesy judgment and destruction. Jonah rejoiced at God's judgments against Ninevah, and then didn't want to prophesy salvation after they had repented before God. Samuel, on the other hand, is a good example of a prophet who was properly balanced between mercy and judgment.

Mercy Executes God's Word. On one occasion, for example, Samuel gave Saul the word of the Lord to go and kill all the Amalekites, including women, children, cattle and everything that breathes (1Sam.15:1-3). When Saul did this, but saved some livestock and the king of Amalek as a prize, Samuel took his sword out and "hewed Agag to pieces before the Lord in Gilgal" (1Sam.15:33).

Prophets are Powerful Intercessors. Yet we see elsewhere that when God told Samuel that Saul had failed and was rejected as Israel's king, "it grieved Samuel; and he cried unto the Lord all night" (1Sam.15:11). Not only was Samuel grieved that Saul had failed, but he cried in grief at the loss of Saul and of the destruction and hurt this had caused the people of God. Mercy and compassion like his are vitally necessary for prophets to function properly as spokesmen for God.

The **spirit of wisdom** is also full of **good fruit**, not just in seed form, but grown to ripeness and maturity that others may eat of it. Nobody wants to eat immature fruit, which is bitter and non-nutritious. So prophets and prophetic people must develop proven, fruitful ministries if they are to be recognized and received, not only as speaking for the Lord, but from the Lord. Nobody will give heed to one who is ill-tempered, lazy, sorrowful and generally lacking in the fruit of the Spirit which all Christians must develop.

Prophetic ministers must also minister such fruit to others **without partiality or hypocrisy**. We must be unbiased and impartial, without religious exclusivism. We cannot be a respecter of persons; we must deal and relate to them all with fairness and equality.

The prophets must be real, genuine people without deception or pretense. Our walk must be the same as our talk, our **manhood** equal to our **ministry**, our **personal life** the same as our **pulpit life.** Are you one person at home or on the job and another at church or in the pulpit?

One question will drive this point home. Of all the prophets, ministers or Church members you know, which one would you want to be your next-door neighbor and closest companion for the first million years of eternity?

Personality of True Prophets. I desire for the prophets to have a greater zeal for a reputation as a man or woman of God than for a name as a great prophetic ministry with signs and wonders. True prophetic ministry, with the wisdom nature of Jesus Christ, will not simply impress people with supernatural manifestations. It will cause people to fall in love with Jesus.

Does your life and ministry portray the personality of Jesus Christ? Could people look at you and say, "Now I know what Jesus is like, not only in His power, but in His personality"?

Faith Which Worketh by Love. Jesus operated in the faith of God and healed the sick, cast out devils, raised the dead and prophesied hope to the humble and correction and judgment to religious hypocrites. Please read 1 Corinthians 13 in several translations to receive the full impact of the reality that God puts much more importance on our spirit and motivation than on our performance.

Verses 1-4 show that we can be the greatest charismatic and gifted prophetic person that ever ministered, yet if we're not motivated and directed by God's love, it profits us nothing. We can be the greatest man or woman of faith that ever worked miracles, but without love it still profits nothing. We can even be the greatest giver of self and finances, but without love it gains us no reward or profit.

Jesus spoke stern words to the religious hypocrites and taught strong, hard truth to His followers, but everything He did was motivated by love—tough "agape" love. Whether something is said or done in love is not determined so much by what we do as by how we do it; not so much by what we say as by what spirit in which we convey it. It must be in the spirit of wisdom and motivated by love.

When I received Prophetic Presbytery in 1953, one of the prophecies stated: *"For lo, the faith that worketh by love shall work mightily in thee. For, to this end hast thou been called, saith the Lord."* The Holy Spirit has faithfully worked over the years to bring this word to pass. Love is a fruit of the Spirit. Gifts are given, but fruit is grown. This prophetic seed, placed in my spirit at an early age, is probably the reason why I have grown up with a burden to make sure that I, and the prophets I influence, faithfully do the work of the prophetic ministry with God's love.

The message may be hard, but the prophet must not be harsh. The prophetic word may be corrective and rebuking, but that does not give the prophet a right to be critical and repulsive in his or her presentation. Based on the three main scriptures which we have just discussed, we must conclude that the spirit of wisdom, love, the beatitudes, the character and personality of

Christ Jesus are all synonymous. Our conclusion is summarized in these alliterated statements:

Wisdom without **love** is Worthless.
Revelation without **wisdom** is Radical.
Ministry without **mercy** is Madness.
Understanding without **love** is Useless.
Spirituality without **love** is a Sham.
Prophetic ministry without **love** is Profitless.
Prophetic song without **love** is Non-Productive.
Faith working without **love** is Fruitless.
Sacrifice without **love** is Senseless.
National Recognition without **love** is Nothing Rewarded.
Success without Christ's **love and wisdom** is Spurious.

The Prophet's Personal Ministry vs. Christ's Corporate Purpose. In light of these purposes and goals of the Prophetic Movement, we must be careful to maintain the proper attitude and spirit in our lives and ministries. Humility will be required for individual ministers to fit into the big picture of God's plans for the Church as a whole.

Paul's analogy of **one human body with many members**— each member having its own unique function—portrays clearly the position of prophetic ministers today. The function of an individual member within a body is not an end in itself; it is a contributing part of the whole. The human body is not made to provide its members a place to function; the individual members are created to function collectively in unity to fulfill the one purpose of the one body. Though the members must each maintain their own life and function, they must not become self-serving independent prophets. They must make sure their ministry interrelates with Christ's overall purpose for His company of prophets. Then they must fit in with God's purpose for His Church and the Church into Christ's eternal purpose (1Cor.12).

A song played on a keyboard provides another useful **analogy.** Each note is not sounded to magnify and bring attention to itself. Rather, it is played with many other notes to create the full song that the Master Musician desires. The restoration of the prophets is the piece of music that Jesus is playing at this time in His orchestration of the restoration of all truth. When He prepares the sheet music for the presentation of His song, He arranges each note to sound forth with exactly the right tone at the right time. And all notes are vital for the song.

When one key goes flat, loses tone or is otherwise out of harmony with the rest, then the Master Tuner must take His instruments and restore it. If the key refuses to be restored, then He replaces it with another. Our humble dedication to God's overall purposes for the Prophetic Movement will enable us to function individually as we were created to function, while contributing uniquely and harmoniously to the song Jesus is singing today. Christ is not raising up just one prophet to magnify His own ministry but a great body of prophets to fulfill His corporate purpose for the Church on planet earth.

Principles for Evaluating Prophets. Over the years I have developed what I call the 10 M's for evaluating all facets of a person's life and ministry. Extensive teaching has been given at the CI Prophets Conferences concerning these ten points. I have a 90 minute cassette teaching tape on these 10 M's. There will be a whole chapter devoted to them in "Prophets 3". I plan, in the near future, to write a small book in order to do justice to all the vital biblical truths related to these ten principles.

The 10 M's are placed here in outline form only to give further insight concerning the proper spirit and motivation of God's true prophets and those who God wants to participate in and propagate the prophetic ministry.

All of our CI-NPM prophetic ministers are required to give an "Evaluation Report Form" to each Pastor where they minister. The Pastor gives an evaluation of how fruitful the CI-NPM minister was in all areas of the 10 M's. When two different Pastors report the same personal weakness or questionable prophetic practice of one of our ministers, then we bring it to their attention. Counsel, wisdom, prayer and encouragement is given to help him or her to strengthen that character or ministerial link in their life. A chain is no stronger than its weakest link. Our prophets, prophetesses and prophetic ministers appreciate this follow up, oversight and accountability in their lives. They are taught to have the Beatitudes of Christ, manifest His powerful prophetic ministry by the faith which works by love, and to allow all their actions and reactions to be directed by the spirit of wisdom. Conscientiously practicing the proper principles of the 10 M's enables a prophet to maintain his ministry in purity and maturity. If we would judge ourselves continually by these 10 M's, we would eliminate much of the judgment from others (ICor.11:31).

10 M's for Judging Prophetic Ministers

1. MANHOOD

Gen.1:26,27	God makes a man before manifesting mighty ministry
Rom.8:29	Man-apart from position, message or ministry
He.2:6,10	Per-son-al-ity-evaluating person not performance
ITim.2:5	Jesus-manhood 30 years; ministry 3 ½; 10 to 1 ratio

2. MINISTRY

2Cor.6:3	No offense to ministry; 1 Cor. 2:4,5 - power & demonstration
Mt.7:15-21	By their fruits you shall know them -anointing, results
Deut.18:22	Prophecies or preaching productive -proven, pure, positive

3. MESSAGE

Eph.4:15	Speak the truth in love; present-truth, and life giving
1Tim.4:2	Message balanced, scriptural, doctrinally and spiritually right
Mk.16:20	God confirms His Word - not person, pride or reputation

4. MATURITY

Jas.3:17	Attitude right; mature in human relations; heavenly wisdom
Gal.5:22	Fruit of spirit, Christlike character, dependable steadfast, He.5:14
1Cor.13	Not childish; Biblically knowledgeable and mature—not a novice.

5. MARRIAGE

1Tim.3:2,5	Scripturally in order. Personal family vs. God's family
1Pet.3:1,7	Priorities straight - God 1st, wife & family, then ministry
Eph.5:22-23	Marriage to exemplify relationship of Christ & His Church

6. METHODS

Tit.1:16	Rigidly righteous, ethical, honest, integrity - upright
Rom.1:18	Not manipulating or deceptive, doesn't speak "evangelistically"
Rom.3:7-8	Good end results do not justify unscriptural methods

7. MANNERS

Tit.1:7;3:1,2	Unselfish, polite, kind, gentleman or lady, discreet
Eph.4:29;5:4	Proper speech and communication in words and mannerism

8. MONEY

1Tim.3:6(AMP)	"Craving wealth and resorting to ignoble and dishonest methods"
1Tim.6:5-17	Lk.12:15 - Love of money and materialism destroys (i.e. Achan)

9. MORALITY

1Cor.6:9-18	Virtuous, pure and proper relationships, Col.3:5
Eph.5:3	Biblical sexual purity in attitude & action, ICor.5:11
Mt.5:28	Wrong thoughts of desire to do - without opportunity to act

10. MOTIVE

Mt.6:1	To serve or to be seen? Fulfill personal drive or God's desire?
1Cor.16:15	True motivation?...To minister or be a Minister?
Pr.16:2	To herald the truth or just to be heard by man?
1Cor.13:1-3	Motivated by God's love or lust for power, fame, name etc.

10

THE PROPHETIC MOVEMENT
VS.
THE NEW AGE MOVEMENT

For every divine reality there is a demonic counterfeit. The supernatural gifts of the Holy Spirit are no exception. For that reason, many Christians are understandably cautious whenever they encounter such phenomena, because they fear that the source might be Satan rather than God.

This is especially so today, when satanic counterfeits of spiritual gifts are common and widely publicized. Unfortunately, some prophetic ministers operating in the Holy Spirit-given gifts of prophecy, the word of knowledge, the word of wisdom, discerning of spirits, or even miracles are sometimes accused of practicing witchcraft, consorting with familiar spirits, or practicing so-called "New Age" techniques. Actually, this is not a new accusation; Christians who spoke in tongues in the early Pentecostal Movement were often accused of demonic activity by their non-Pentecostal brothers and sisters in Christ who pointed out that some pagan religions practice speaking in tongues.

Surface Similarities. No doubt similarities appear **on the surface** between much that is done by the Spirit of God and much that the devil does as a counterfeit through people involved in cults, the occult, witchcraft, Eastern religions, Satan worship and the New Age Movement. The devil's tricks are able to mimic tongues, prophecy, words of knowledge and wisdom, and even miracles, including apparent healings. And no wonder: Familiar spirits can convey information supernaturally, and Satan can call on his demons to perform feats such as levitation and psychic phenomenon. He can presumably even command an obedient spirit of infirmity to pause its harassment of an individual to make it appear that a supernatural healing has taken place.

Nevertheless, these are only superficial similarities. The source of a supernatural phenomenon is what determines its legitimacy. Is it from the Spirit of God or from Satan? From the Spirit of truth or from the spirit of error?

Real vs. Counterfeit. As an illustration, consider a parallel example: the counterfeit dollar bill. If the counterfeiter has done his job well, you can hold a real bill right next to the fake one, and only someone trained to detect the difference will be able to do so. The two bills will look just alike, and the fake bill will even buy goods from those who are deceived by it. It is interesting to note that the government trains their people to detect the counterfiet currency, not by examining the false, but by constantly handling and working with actual government published dollars. The best way to train God's people to discern the false is to constantly keep them exposed to and involved in the true supernatural ministry.

So what is the difference between the real and the counterfeit bill? It is not in appearance; they look almost exactly alike. It is not even in function; in most situations the counterfeit bill can function just as well as the real bill, buying goods for the person who knowingly or unknowingly uses it.

No, the difference between a real bill and a counterfeit bill is in their **source.** The real money originates in the presses of the U.S. government, and thus carries a value, legitimacy and authority granted to it by that government. The counterfeit, however, originates in an illegitimate press with the purpose of circumventing the value and authority of the real. The real money is backed up by hard cash in the government treasury (or at least we hope so!); the other is backed up only by the deceit and greed of criminals.

So it is with counterfeit spiritual gifts. A New Age channeler may give an accurate word of knowledge; a palm reader or psychic may predict the future; a Hindu shaman may relieve someone's symptoms of physical affliction; a yoga practioner may levitate. But this does not mean that a Christian who prophesies, gives words of knowledge or wisdom, or works miracles is relying on demons. The existence of the counterfeit only demonstrates that there is a reality to be counterfeited. There are no counterfeit three dollar bills, because there are no real ones.

Discern Through Teaching and Spirit. For that reason, we must distinguish between the real and counterfeit in supernatural gifts by examining the **teaching and spirit** of those who are practicing the gifts. A true prophetic minister used by God will not contradict in his or her teaching the Logos Word of God. Especially in matters which are central to Christian teaching (as opposed to matters such as eschatology or denominational differences), the true prophetic minister will affirm the biblical teaching of the Church with regard to the nature of God and the salvation offered in Jesus Christ (Deut.13:1-3).

With that in mind, we should be able to identify those whose source of power is not God. Though they may use biblical language, they will sooner or later reveal their origins by contradicting or challenging essential truths of the Christian faith.

Common New Age Teachings. The most common sign of a teaching that is cultic, occultic, New Age, or otherwise counterfeit is the notion that **God is impersonal**—that God is in everything, or that God is everything and everything is God. This idea is at the heart of New Age teaching, leading that movement's followers to believe that they themselves are God and can draw on their own power from being one with the cosmos.

Christians, of course, insist instead that the universe is God's **creation**—something separate and apart from God that He made out of nothing. We are not God. Rather, as Spirit-filled believers we have the Spirit of God residing in us, and it is **His** power and **His** gifts that allow us to minister supernaturally, according to **His** divine enablements and directives.

A second typical sign of cultic, occult, or New Age teaching is the **denial of the uniqueness of Christ and His saving death and resurrection.** In the New Age Movement, Jesus is seen as an "enlightened teacher" or "spiritual master," but not as the unique Son of God. Since the earliest years of the Church, the devil has tried to counterfeit Christian doctrine with teachings that Jesus was not divine; or that He was not the unique, only-begotten Son of God; or that He was never really human; or that He was not really resurrected from the grave.

Jesus is the Only Way, Truth and Life. No matter how accurate or powerful a person may be in supernatural activity, if that person denies that Jesus is the unique Son of God, who came in the flesh to redeem us by His shed blood, and who rose again to reign forever, then that person is not operating by the Spirit of God. A true prophetic minister will affirm the truth of Christ's unique atonement (1Jn.4:1).

A third area of doctrinal error among New Age and other counterfeit groups is the insistence that **good and evil are one**, that there is no ultimate right or wrong, and that humanity does not need to be redeemed from bondage to the devil and its own fallen, sinful nature. New Agers in particular may speak of "sin," but they mean by that word what the ancient Gnostic heretics meant in New Testament times: They believe that "sin" is not separation from God through wrongdoing, but rather that it is failure to recognize our own divinity through ignorance.

That is why the New Age Movement places such emphasis on mystical experiences, trances, "channeling," and dealings with spirits: They see such experiences as a means to convince people that they are "God," that the universe is mystically "one," and that God-like power and knowledge are available inside them.

True prophetic ministers of God, on the other hand, affirm the biblical truth that "all have sinned and come short of the glory of God" (Rom.3:23). And when they say "sin," they mean willful turning away from God—not ignorance.

God's true Prophetic Movement, then, is not at all New

Age, cultic, occultic, or satanic, and it should not be confused with these non-Christian groups. The devil may be able to mimic the work of the Holy Spirit, but the source of knowledge and power for true prophetic ministers is God Himself. Pharaoh's sorcerers had the power to duplicate Moses' supernatural sign of turning the rod into a snake. But however similar certain phenomena may seem, the difference in their origin is the critical difference. Those who truly belong to God's restoration movement today will give all the glory to God for whatever is accomplished through their ministry (Ex.7:10-12).

Trust God for the Real Thing. If we are reluctant to practice the gifts ourselves because we fear that we may be drawing on Satan's power rather than God's, we should simply commit our ministry to God in prayer, asking His Spirit to minister through us and binding any other spirit from doing so. Then we must minister in faith that God has indeed answered our prayer.

People who want to be baptized in the Holy Spirit and speak in tongues often have the same fear. They ask, "What if I receive a counterfeit instead of the real thing? How do I know that my prayer language is of God instead of the devil or the flesh?"

The answer given to them is usually that they must trust God's fatherly character and willingness to answer their prayer, blessing them with what they need. In Jesus' words, they must have faith that God loves us so much, He would not give us a "stone" if we ask for "bread" (Mt.7:9-11; Lk.11:11-13). So they can receive the gift of tongues and practice it in confidence, having faith that after praying for the Holy Spirit, God would not send them a demon instead!

The same is true of those who desire to be used in prophetic ministry. If they commit their ministry each time to the Lord, asking for the Holy Spirit to speak through them and binding any other spirit from doing so, then they can rest in a confidence that God will not allow the devil to use them instead. And if they operate under the training and supervision of proven, Godly prophetic ministers, in cooperation with them, they can minimize the chance of mistakes being made in the prophetic ministry.

11

GOD'S STANDARD: HIS PROPHETS AND PROPHETIC CHURCH

Deuteronomy 18:9-22 gives God's reason why He placed the sentence of eternal judgment upon the "ite" tribes of Canaan and gave Israel the divine commission to annihilate them utterly:

> When you enter the land which the Lord your God gives you, you shall not learn to imitate the detestable things of those nations. There shall not be found among you anyone who makes his son or his daughter pass through the fire, one who uses divination, one who practices witchcraft, or one who interprets omens or a sorcerer, or one who casts a spell, or a medium, or a spiritist, or one who calls up the dead. *For whoever does these things is detestable to the Lord, and because of these detestable things the Lord your God will drive them out before you.* You shall be blameless before the Lord your God. For those nations, which you shall dispossess, listen to those who practice witchcraft and to diviners, but as for you, the Lord your God has not allowed you to do so. The Lord your God will raise up for you a prophet like me from among you, from your countrymen, you shall listen to him (Deut.18:9-16, NASB).

Prophets are God's Standard for Supernatural Communications. (Amos 3:7) The amplified Bible gives footnote comments on these scriptures in Deuteronomy concerning "that **order**

of true prophets whom God commissioned in unbroken succession to instruct, direct and warn His people." It says that "in this view the gist of [the message] is, There is **no need to consult with diviners and soothsayers,** for I shall afford you the benefit of **divinely appointed prophets.**"

The "prophet like unto Moses" is speaking primarily of Jesus the coming Messiah. Jesus fulfilled that prophecy and He was God's special appointed prophet, but now that the Messiah prophet has fulfilled His personal, earthly, prophetic commission, He is raising up a company of prophets to become His standard for supernatural communications from God to humanity, heaven to earth, spiritual realm to natural realm.

All other realms of supernatural spirit information and communications are an abomination to God, and He detests them so much that His wrath is eventually poured out upon all who practice such things. Occultists, wizards, witches and spiritists have practiced divination and consulted familiar spirits throughout all the world down through the ages. But today there has arisen a demonic spiritist movement causing intensified activity of the occult and satanism with human sacrifices.

This movement is spreading now like wildfire in America, preying on the innocent and ignorant. It is invading high society and the financial world in a milder form in the New Age movement. But whether we are talking about black or white magicians, witches or New Agers, God utterly hates all their practices. He wants them exposed for what they are and driven out of His land.

God Still Hates False Spirit Communications. Eternal God has not changed His attitude nor His decree against such practices since the day He declared these things to Israel thirty-five hundred years ago. The only difference is that back then they were to be physically killed, and prophets who prophesied inaccurately were to be stoned to death. Today, the weapons of our warfare are not carnal, but mighty in the Spirit to the pulling down of these spiritist strongholds; and prophets are not physically killed for inaccurate prophecy (2Cor.10:4-6).

In response to the false communication channelers, God's true prophets are arising today. God's answer then was the ministry of the **prophet**, and His solution is still the same today. The opposing forces are being set in battle array, and when the battle is over only one group will be left in the land (Ps.37:9-29).

God declares that the righteous shall inherit the land and the wicked shall be cut off. There will not only be battles fought in intercessory prayer, warfare praise and prophetic praying and praising; there will also be public confrontations between these two opposing forces. The present-day Elijah company of prophets are being prepared to meet publicly with these false prophets just as Elijah met with Jezebel's false Baal prophets on Mount Carmel (1Ki.18; Acts 13:10,11)

Nationwide Televised Confrontation. They will probably meet in contexts such as nationwide television talk shows. It will be a spiritual battle that will make the hair on the back of your neck stand up and chill bumps run all over your body. The spiritual powers of darkness and God's anointed prophets and apostles will meet face-to-face in a powerful confrontation to determine who really is the God of heaven and earth: humanity, Satan or Jesus Christ.

It will be like the days when the prophet Moses went before Pharaoh and declared that Jehovah, the Great I AM is the true God of all natural things and heavenly realms. The wizards, witches and satanists will be able to turn their sticks into snakes like Moses did. It will look at first as if the Church prophets of God can do no more than the warlocks and witches.

But God's miraculous power will increase in the prophets until the Creator himself will arise in them and speak His creative word that can turn dust into living lice. After the third encounter, the magicians and diviners were no match for God's prophet Moses, and the same will be true of God's prophets today (Exodus 5-12).

The prophets are arising and will continue to increase in Godly purity and power until all false communication channels are exposed for the false and wicked system that they are. The

President of the United States and heads of nations will begin to seek out the Christian prophets and prophetic ministers to find out what is really taking place and to know what to do. World conditions will come to the place that human hearts will be failing for fear.

The manipulators that control the economy, stock market and world banking systems will lose their control. God will cut their puppet strings and take things out of their hands. Only those who know how to hear and speak the true mind of Christ and the Word of God will have the answers.

The Joseph and Daniel prophetic company will arise with the supernatural answers for the needs of the Egyptian Pharaohs and Babylonian empires of this world. The prophetic Church will finally demonstrate fully that Jesus Christ really is the answer for the world—not only to save them from their sins, but to bring peace on earth and goodwill toward all people.

God has forever established that there is only one door to heaven and one mediator between God and humanity, and that is the man Christ Jesus (1Tim.2:5). If anyone, New Ager or otherwise, tries to come through any other way, he or she is looked upon as a thief and robber (Jn.10:7,9). There is only one means of communication between God and humanity, heaven and earth, natural realm and spiritual realm.

Religious Witchcraft. It is just as wrong to try contacting or communing with God through mother Mary or departed saints as it is to try through human physic, occultic or satanic means. Witchcraft is wrong whether it is Charismatic or Catholic religious witchcraft or occultic or New Age witchcraft. God will only sanction and work with that which is in Jesus Christ and His divinely designated representatives.

The fivefold ministry is an extension of the ministry of Jesus Christ upon planet earth. The **prophets** have the burden, responsibility, anointing and privilege to **represent Jesus as the true prophet**. The **apostles** also have a kindred ministry in this supernatural revelation knowledge realm. The prophets and apostles have the responsibility to equip the Church to be a prophetic and apostolic Church that can move in the super-natural power of God to represent Jesus Christ fully and to demonstrate the kingdom of God on earth until His kingdom has come and His will is done on earth as it is in heaven (Mt.6:10).

The Greatest Indication of Where the Church is. God's bringing forth of the company of prophets to expose and drive out the false prophetic communicators in the land is the greatest sign of the times concerning where the Church is in its restorational journey from worldly Egypt to its promised Canaan land. The restoration of the prophet ministry is the greatest indication that the Church has now prophetically crossed over Jordan and entered its warfare to drive out the inhabitants of the land upon whom God has pronounced eternal judgment because of their detestable practices.

Some will be driven out by believing the gospel message, being born-again and becoming one with God's prophetic people. Others will cease their practices after they become enlightened to the error of their ways. Still others will set themselves against God and His prophets and war against them.

God's judgment will fall upon this last group, and many will die or suffer horrible things, whether they are religious false prophets, humanists, psychics, or satanists. God will purge His floor (earth is his footstool): The wheat of righteous people He will gather into His garner, but the chaff of the false He will burn with unquenchable fire. For our God is a consuming fire. The prophets are now beginning to proclaim "the day of vengeance of our God," and "the coming of the great and dreadful day of the Lord" (Mal.4:5; Is.61:2; He.12:29; Mt.3:12; Ps.149:6-9; Mal. 3:16-4:3; Mt.5:35; 22:44) (see point 7 in chapter 13 for numerous scriptures on saints executing God's eternal judgments).

12

WHAT WILL THE ROLE OF THE PROPHETS BE?

As we look forward to the full blossoming of the Prophetic Movement in the years to come, we need an understanding of the restored role of the prophet in the Church to help us avoid misunderstandings and extremes. In particular, we need insight into the nature of the prophet, the necessity of prophets today, the appropriate place of personal prophecy, the relation of prophets to doctrine and the relationship of the prophet to the other fivefold ministers.

The Nature of a Prophet. First of all, who is a prophet and what is his or her ministry? A prophet is just a person who has been divinely gifted with the nature and ability of Christ the Prophet. Jesus was able to receive the mind and purposes of God His Father and know what was in the heart of human beings through His office of the prophet. His ability to know the counsels and purposes of God for an individual life, such as He revealed to Peter (Jn.21:15-23), was an ability that came from His ministry as a prophet.

When Christ Jesus calls and gifts a man or woman with that part of His ability, attributes and divine nature, then that person has been commissioned to the office of a prophet. Prophets will always have an ability to prophesy. They will vary in their gifts of the Holy Spirit, but they primarily move in the gifts of prophecy, word of knowledge, word of wisdom, discerning of spirits and sometimes healing. The typical prophet moves more in prophecy, word of knowledge and word of wisdom.

Ministers and other saints who are not called to the office of a prophet may manifest one or more of these gifts, but there is a difference in their anointing, authority and level of function. A saint manifesting the gift of prophecy to a congregation is limited to the general activity of that gift, which is edification, exhortation and comfort (1Cor.14:3).

The prophet, when ministering with his or her gifted office and prophetic anointing, has the same authority for reproving, correcting, directing and instructing in the rhema word of the Lord as the other four ministers have in their teaching, counseling and preaching with the Logos Word.

How Does Someone Become a Prophet? A person does not call or appoint him or herself to any of the ascension gift ministries. This is strictly the personal prerogative and gift of Christ Himself. Each minister needs to know what his or her ascension gift office is in the Body of Christ.

After years of research, life experience, scriptural study and personal involvement in the ministry, I have concluded that a person is only called and gifted to one of the five administrative offices of apostle, prophet, evangelist, pastor or teacher. Some other ministers believe that you graduate from one fivefold ministry to another and I grant allowance for that possibility. That person may be required to do the work and fill the position of any of the other four at one time or another in his or her life. These other ministerial activities will be used by the Lord to mature that person in his or her specific calling.

Consider two examples from Scripture. Jeremiah was called to be a prophet from his mother's womb (Jer.1:5). In the case of Paul, numerous scriptures state that he was "called to be an apostle" ten of his epistles begin with a statement acknowledging his call to be an apostle (for example, Eph.1:1; Col.1:1). He exhibited the fruit of an apostle; yet he also held evangelistic campaigns and itinerated from church to church. He pastored for several years some of the churches that were established out of his ministry. He taught the Word of God better than most, and even wrote fourteen divinely inspired letters that became books of the New Testament. Despite these ministries, however, he never states that he was ever called to be a pastor, teacher, evangelist, or prophet. He does declare that he was ordained as an apostle to be a preacher and a teacher of the Gentiles (1Tim.2:7; 2Tim.1:11).

One Calling or Many? When Paul was itinerating from church to church on his second journey, we would have introduced him in modern church terminology as "our visiting evangelist" or "Evangelist Paul." When he stayed in one church and taught them daily for several months, we would have referred to him as "our teacher." While he was taking the oversight of one of the churches for several months we would have referred to him as "Pastor Paul."

The fact remains, however, that though he did the ministerial work of evangelizing, teaching and pastoring—and even at times he functioned like a prophet—he had one Christ-gifted calling, that of the **apostle**. Each minister has one specific gifted calling but may perform many of the fivefold ministerial functions.

My Personal Experience. Probably one of the reasons for this conclusion is that my personal experience bears this principle out. I pastored for six years, then travelled for three years in full-time evangelism, then taught in a Bible College for five years, then founded and established the Christian International School of Theology during the mid-1960's.

I have received personal prophecies from many other people over the last thirty-eight years. Those which were recorded total over seven hundred pages of typewritten prophecies containing over a hundred and seventy-five thousand words—enough to fill three volumes the size of this book.

These prophecies have not been from just one place or people. They have been received while ministering on almost every continent of the world. These words were prophesied by ministers representing all fivefold ascension gift ministries; by new converts, and by ministers who have been ordained for over fifty years; by male and female; by old and young.

The prophecies have come from Christians in the historic denominational churches, classical Pentecostal churches, and different "camps" and fellowships including those called by the names "Restoration," "Charismatic," "Faith," and "Kingdom." They have come from Christian men's and women's organizations such as the Full Gospel Businessmen's Fellowship International and Ladies' Aglow. And they have come from special ministry groups such as Teen Challenge and Maranatha Ministries.

The amazing thing is that in all of these thousands of prophetic words through hundreds of people from all over the world during four decades, there has been no statement to contradict my office and calling of prophet as God sovereignly declared it in the beginning. It is true that just within this last decade I have received about fifteen prophecies concerning an "apostolic anointing" and my doing "the work of an apostle." But none have mentioned the calling of an apostle.

An Apostolic-Prophet. But The Holy Spirit prophetically stated that this apostolic anointing was being granted for two reasons. The first reason was that I had been faithful in multiplying the prophet anointing that had been given, so now that anointing was being doubled by the addition of the apostolic anointing (Mt.25:28,29). The second reason was that the apostolic anointing had been given for the purpose of pioneering, establishing and taking a fatherhood responsibility for the restoration and propagation of the office of the prophet. That is one reason why the term apostolic-prophet is used to describe my present ministerial position in the Body of Christ, specifically as it relates to my position of oversight of the CI-NPM.

Prophets and the Written Word. Once we understand the nature of the prophet, we must consider the basic issue of the need for prophets in the Church today. Some theologians question whether or not there is even a place in the modern Church for prophets. They believe that we have no use for prophets today because we now have the Bible. The Bible, they say, reveals all of God's principles, ways, wisdom, word, direction and revealed will for every person.

Logos Word vs. Prophet's Rhema Word. To respond we need only ask a question: If a divinely inspired book of instruction eliminates the need for the prophet, then why didn't God do away with the office and ministry of the prophet after Moses wrote the Pentateuch (the first five books of the Bible?)

The Pentateuch contains the Law of God with detailed instructions for every area of human life. Yet even though Israel had the Law, God still continued to raise up prophets to give specific messages to leaders, nations and individuals. The priests and Levites taught the written Word of God, but the prophets did more than read and teach the written Word—the Logos. They spoke God's present rhema word to specific situations and needs.

In fact, the prophets were more numerous and ministered more during the fifteen centuries of the Law than during any other time in biblical history. Yet for that period of time, the Law of Moses was the complete revealed will of God, even down to the very details of humankind's relationship to each other and to God. It was the complete written Word, the Logos for the children of Israel during the dispensation of the Law just as the New Testament is for the dispensation of the Church. In both dispensations, God's prophets are needed.

Does the Holy Spirit Replace the Prophet? Some theologians imply that the Church does not need the ministry of the prophet today because the Holy Spirit has been sent. Each Christian now has the Holy Spirit within, they insist, and He illuminates them with a rhema when needed. Consequently, the prophet with a rhema is no longer needed, except as an inspired preacher expounding upon the already-revealed and written Word of God.

If we accepted that idea as proper theology, then it would be more realistic to say that we do not need **teachers** to teach the Word of God, because each Church Age saint has the Holy Spirit and a Bible. The Bible is self-explanatory and there are numerous scriptures which state that the Holy Spirit shall teach you all things, lead you into all truth, take the things of Christ and show them to you, and be your illuminator, director, counselor and enabler (Jn.16:7-15).

1John 2:27 states, "But the anointing which you have received of him abides in you, and you need not that any man teach you." It would be much easier to make a theological argument for doing away with the office of the teacher in the Body of Christ than that of the **prophet**.

If prophets are not needed in Christ's Church because we now have the revealed will of God written for all to read, and the Holy Spirit to personalize that Word when needed, then the same reasoning would have to eliminate from the Church not only the teacher, but eventually also all the other fivefold ministers. They could say we do not need the **evangelist**; we can just give everyone a Bible and let the Holy Spirit do the work of convicting and converting. Likewise, the Church would not need **apostles** to do their founding and establishing ministry, because the Church has already been established by the original twelve apostles. Nor would the Church need **pastors**, for the Holy Spirit and the Bible will give direction, and Jesus is the Good Shepherd to every one of His sheep.

The Fivefold Ministers Are Still Needed. Nevertheless, the biblical fact is that the Word of God emphatically states that the resurrected Christ gifted individuals to be **apostles, prophets, evangelists, pastors and teachers.** There is not one scriptural indication anywhere that any of the five have been recalled, dispensationally depleted, or removed from their Christ-appointed ministry to the Church throughout her existence on earth. Ephesians 4:12 declares that the fivefold representation, manifestation and personified ministry of Christ in mortal bodies will continue until every member in the Body of Christ is fully matured and equipped in their ministries so that the whole body is edified, built up and matured (Eph. 4:11-13).

Only as all five of the ascension gift ministers equally and fully function in the Church will she enter her predestined purpose of coming into the "unity of the faith, and of the knowledge of the son of God, unto a perfect man, unto the measure of the stature of the fullness of Christ.... [and] by speaking the truth in love [she] may grow up into him in all things, which is the head, even Christ" (vv.13,15).

Prophets Are Perpetual. Each age, dispensation and covenant of God has added and dropped terminology concerning certain ministries. There was first the time of the patriarchs. Then the Law defined priests, Levites, scribes and kings. In the New Testament we have mention of apostles, prophets, evangelists, pastors, teachers, elders, deacons, bishops and saints.

We should note here that the only ministry which can be found **consistently functioning in every age and dispensation from Genesis to Revelation** is that of the **prophet**. The prophet is the one ministry that has never been limited to any particular dispensation, age, or covenant of God. The man or woman who becomes the pure expression of the mind of God to humankind is the ministry mentioned and manifest more consistently throughout the whole Bible. And that ministry is the **prophet**.

When, Where and to Whom Personal Prophecy May Be Ministered. Not long ago someone suggested to me that neither prophets nor prophetic ministers nor prophetic presbyteries should prophesy over anyone unless they had a letter of authorization from their pastor. He insisted that no one should receive ministry from anyone unless his or her pastor is present or gives authorization.

If such a requirement were a biblical divine order—if God required that church members have a letter from the pastor for approval for members to go to a conference or seminar of another person or ministry—then that would apply to all church members in all churches including all Catholics, Fundamentalists, Pentecostals and Charismatics. That would mean that Billy Graham should make sure each person attending his evangelistic crusade has a letter of authorization from his or her pastor before he allows his workers to minister to that person and lead him or her into a new spiritual experience of being born-again, an experience of which many priests and pastors do not approve because it is not a part of their church doctrine or practice.

The same would be true of a Baptist church member attending a charismatic conference of an FGBMFI chapter meeting or conference. How many of the present Charismatic Christians who were in Catholic, Historic Protestant and Evangelical churches would have been exposed to and received the gift of the Holy Spirit with speaking in other tongues if they had to obtain a letter of approval from their pastor or priest?

The Situation Is The Same As With Earlier Movements. Some Pentecostal and Charismatic pastors would say, "But participating in the prophetic movement is different from participating in our movement."Some insist that ministering personal prophecy to other pastors' church members brings confusion to them and disrupts their faithfulness and contentment to be a church member in their home church. But if a Charismatic pastor thinks that ministering the born-again esperience to a Catholic or baptism of the Holy Spirit to a Fundamentalist doesn't bring confusion and disrupt a person's contentment to be in their home church, that pastor has only to ask the Catholic priest or Evangelical pastor of those members who received a born-again experience at a Billy Graham meeting or speaking in tongues at a Charismatic conference.

Some pastors who believe in personal prophecy have stated that since they themselves provide prophetic presbytery for their people, then it is out of order for them to receive personal prophecy from someone who is not their spiritual covering and authority in their lives. They have stated that it would be wrong for them to receive prophetic presbytery or a word from a prophet if the pastor has not authorized it.

Ministerial Ethics Must be the Same for All Ministers. If that is proper ministerial ethics, divine order and biblical principle, then does that mean that a Pentecostal pastor is justified in saying that no minister at an FGBMFI meeting or a Charismatic pastor has any right to minister the Holy Spirit with speaking in other tongues to one of his or her church members? Can the Pentecostal pastor rightfully call the Charismatic pastor or FGBMFI president and rebuke him or her for being unethical and out of divine order by ministering the Holy Spirit to someone that way?

He could say, "We have special services in our own church where we minister the Holy Spirit gift to our people. I do not want other ministers laying hands on my members and ministering to them. I do not want them instructing my members on how to receive the Holy Spirit and how to minister it to others." The Pentecostal pastor could say that because these ministers had ministered spiritual things to his or her people without a pastor's letter of authorization, then the other ministry should be branded and put off limits because they were not operating in divine order, proper church structure, or ministerial ethics.

Must Oral Roberts have local pastoral approval to lay hands on local church members and minister divine healing to them? If this is a divine biblical principle, then Oral Roberts has broken it a million times, for he has laid hands on over a million people, most of whom were not his own church members.

Charismatics Were Baptized Outside of Their Churches. Most present-day Charismatics that received the gift of the Holy Spirit in the 60's and 70's did not receive it in their own local denominational church. Most received it while attending an FGBMFI meeting in a hotel ballroom or at a Charismatic conference. If this idea of having local pastor approval before members can visit another ministry or receive ministry had been strictly followed in the Charismatic movement, then a great majority of those who became "tongues talkers" would not be Charismatics today.

Each church member and minister will have to determine whether this idea is a divine biblical principle or a fear and control tactic of past movement leaders to keep their people from being exposed to a new restorational truth movement which they do not understand. There are only three options for our response to new truth: We can persecute it, be passive about it, or participate and propagate it.

Prophets, Prophecy and Doctrine. Those who have been involved in prophetic ministry for decades have discovered several guidelines with regard to prophets and doctrine.

First of all, fivefold ministers are the headship directors for establishing biblical principles, teachings and Church doctrine. New Testament doctrine was established by proper revelation and application of the Logos Scriptures. Church order, doctrine and practices were not established by prophecy, visions, dreams, or personal spiritual experiences of a private individual (2Pet.1:20). No doubt these may be biblical ministries and experiences that the Holy Spirit can use to gain our attention, enlighten our understanding, or prepare us to receive a doctrine that God is about to reveal. But such personal spiritual experiences should not be the basis for formulating a doctrine.

The Church Council at Jerusalem. Consider the example of the first Church council in Jerusalem, which met to resolve the doctrinal issue concerning whether Gentile Christians should be required to follow the Abrahamic covenant and Mosaic law of circumcision. God's process for the acceptance and establishment of this doctrine was as follows: First, Peter received a vision while praying that adjusted his attitude and opened up his spirit to do something different. Then he went to Cornelius' Gentile household in obedience to the vision and personal rhema word of God and the coinciding invitation of the two men sent by Cornelius who had been instructed by an angel to do so (Acts 10:1-11:18).

The sovereign spiritual experience of Cornelius' household —receiving the forgiveness of sins and the gift of the Holy Spirit, evidenced by speaking in unknown tongues just as the Jewish Christians had—convinced Peter they should also be baptized in water in the name of their new-found Lord and Savior, Jesus Christ. Then Paul and Barnabas started traveling together in ministry. Many more Gentiles began to receive salvation, the gift of Holy Spirit, healing and miracles without becoming proselyte Jews first.

At the council in Jerusalem, Peter gave his testimony of his vision and angelic visitation and the sovereign move of God at Cornelius' house. Barnabas and Paul gave their testimony of the Holy Spirit sovereignly bestowing on the Gentiles all the benefits of Christianity apart from the Mosaic law. These testimonies, visions and supernatural experiences were eye-openers and served as a witness and confirming evidence. But it was not until James received a revelation and application of the Logos that the issue was settled and written into established doctrine for the New Testament Church (Acts 15:1-35).

One Person Cannot Dictate Doctrine. No one man or ministry should establish a doctrine as essential belief and practice for all Christians. Paul declared that he received his revelation on this matter directly from God in the Arabian desert and was not given this truth from the original apostles. But he did not preach it as Church doctrine and send letters to establish it until he had met with the apostles and other fivefold ministers. None of us should ever think ourselves so great or sovereign in the Body of Christ that we believe there is no need to submit our teachings and beliefs to other key present-truth apostles, prophets and other fivefold ministries (Gal.1:11-18).

Church Councils to Come in the 90's. I personally believe that in the 1990's, as prophets and apostles are being restored back to proper order and function within the Church, many of these Church councils of leading present-truth ministers will be necessary. One particular apostle or prophet or camp will never receive the whole revelation for the establishing of prophets and apostles back into the Church.

Many will have visions (even of Jesus), dreams, rhemas, angelic visitations and supernatural personal experiences and sovereign moves of the Holy Spirit in their meetings. But doctrines that claim to be binding on all Christians must not be established by any one apostle, prophet, or camp. There must be meetings of a Church council with other leaders of past and present restorational streams of truth.

Five Principles for Establishing Doctrine. When the fivefold ministers come together to consider doctrines and practices this way, they will need to keep in mind several areas of insight: (1) the claimed revelation from God; (2) the fruit of the ministry among those who have received the doctrine or practice; (3) the supernatural working of God accompanying it; (4) the Logos and rhema word of God application and authority for the doctrine or practice; and (5) the witness of the Spirit and the unified consent of those present.

No Popes. In the meantime, we may say, "As for me and my house"—declaring what our own fellowship or family will believe and practice. But we must not present it in such a way to imply that those who do not believe and worship the same way are out of order or in error. This is not the prerogative of one person—neither the Catholic Pope nor a Charismatic, Kingdom, Faith, or Prophetic Pope.

Each person and fellowship has a responsibility to follow their own revelations, convictions and practices, but not to impose them upon the corporate Body of Christ. Such presumptuous declarations, teachings and actions cause divisions in the Body of Christ. Every erroneous Christian religious group has established certain doctrines and practices that are unique with themselves. This then makes them an exclusive, seclusive, "elected" group that sees itself as superior to all others.

Exclusivism Leads to Cults. The manifestations of this attitude are seen in the extreme groups that arose during the time of the Holiness and Pentecostal movements: Mormons, Christian Scientists, Jehovah's Witnesses. But sad to say, there are also some on the extreme right that are still counted as "mainline" Christian denominations who believe they are the only true people of God. They base this conviction on certain baptism formulas, ways of worship, church order, or some other unique doctrine or practice.

No One Man or Group has it All. The New Testament Scriptures emphatically and repeatedly declare that Christ has only one Church here on planet earth. Not any denomination, fellowship, or restoration camp make up the entirety of that Church. Every truly born-again, blood-washed, sanctified child of God is a member of Christ's Church. They may be Charismatic Catholics, Evangelicals, Pentecostals or Present-truth Prophetic People. We are only parts of the whole and members in particular of the corporate Body of Christ.

All truth and life is found in the whole, not in any one particular part or member. We need each other and will never come to maturity and fullness of truth without each other. The new wine is in the cluster—not just in one individual grape (Is.65:8).

The Relationship of the Prophet to the Other Fivefold Ministers. The Lord revealed to me in the mid-1980's that many extremes would come in the swing of the pendulum of restoration truth concerning prophets and apostles. So I have been making an intensified study throughout Scripture, Church history and present-day writings, joined with much prayer for illumination and even revelation from Christ concerning His proper order for the function and interrelationship of His fivefold ministers.

Most of the writings and teachings of this century are based only on the knowledge and experience of our present limited status—that is, with the Church only recognizing three of the five offices: pastor, evangelist and teacher. All present ministerial church order, structure and relationship has been determined by that perspective. Now, however, sufficient room and proper structure must be made for the function and ministry of the **apostles** and **prophets**.

We Have Not Passed This Way Before. All present-day ministers, and especially those who will be moving in present-truth revelation, must be open, teachable and adjustable to the Holy Spirit's educating us more perfectly in this way. We must follow the admonition of Joshua to the leaders and people of Israel when they were about to enter their promised Canaan Land. They were to sanctify themselves and watch for the moving of the ark of God by the priest. Then, when they saw it begin to move, they were to "go after it!" (Josh.3:1-3).

Joshua emphasized that they had to follow the leadership who was following the Lord so that they might know the way that they must go, **"for ye have not passed this way heretofore"** (v.4). In the same way, we the present-day Church have never passed this way in the history of the restoration of the Church. We have never functioned with the full restoration of all five offices—apostles, prophets, evangelists, pastors and teachers.

One Ministry Restored Each Decade. We said in an earlier chapter that the Holy Spirit had been commissioned to bring all five of Christ's ascension gift ministries to proper order, authority, position and ministry. We also noted that the last fifty years of the twentieth century was designated as the time for that to be accomplished, with each ten-year period being used to restore one of the five.

During that decade a particular ascension gift ministry would be brought forth to be clarified, amplified and magnified within the Church. That fivefold ministry would be brought forth in one decade and fully established within the Church during the following decade. Then each ministry restored would continue to grow and function until it was fully understood, accepted and established in its God-ordained role.

The First Shall Be Last and the Last, First. God revealed to me the reason for choosing the particular order in which He was restoring the fivefold ministers. His divine principle of "the **first**

shall be **last** and the **last, first**" has determined the order of restoration (Mt.19:30; 20:16; 1Cor.12:28).

When God **first** set the fivefold ministers in the Church, His chronological order of establishing them was this: first apostles, second prophets, third teachers, fourth pastors and fifth evangelists. Now during these five decades of reestablishing the fivefold ministries and setting them back in proper order, the Holy Spirit is starting with the **last** that was established and is step-by-step working His way back to the **first**: first, the **evangelist** in the 1950's; second, the **pastor** in the 1960's; third, the **teacher** in the 1970's; fourth, the **prophet** in the 1980's; and finally, the **apostle** in the 1990's.

God's First Order of Establishing the Fivefold. When Christ originally established the ascension gift ministries in the Church, first came the **apostles** who followed Jesus for over three years. Second, the New Testament **prophets** were brought forth, and together, the two foundational ministries of the apostle and prophet, laid the foundation of the Church with proper structure doctrinally and spiritually. Third, the **teachers** were set in to ground the saints in these truths until they were fully established as New Testament churches. **Apostle and prophet teams** then set **pastoral elders** over the churches to guard, feed and lead the flock of believers like a shepherd (Acts 15:32; 16:4,18,25; 2Cor.1:19; 2Th.1:1; Acts 20:28).

After the churches were doctrinally founded and structured into proper church order with a pastor, elders and deacons, then **evangelists** were sent out from the local church. They were sent forth by the Holy Spirit from the local church in a way similar to how Philip, "the deacon turned into an evangelist," went out from the church in Jerusalem to Samaria and conducted that great evangelistic campaign. The evangelists not only went to unreached areas but they also went to churches to encourage the saints and to keep them renewed in Christ's final commission on world evangelism and making disciples in all nations (Acts 6:5; 8:5; Mt.28:19).

No Perfect Structure Until Apostles Restored. God's divine order and structure for the functioning, authority and relationship of fivefold ministry will not be fully revealed and established until after that fifty-year period has brought forth the full restoration and unity of all five ministers. The reality of this revelation implies that not one minister alive today sees the whole picture in proper perspective. We each have and demonstrate only different pieces of the puzzle.

The whole will not be fully seen, understood and established until every puzzle piece is placed in the picture. Only Jesus has the box cover with the whole picture on it. We are individual pieces in the box and on the table. The **pastor, evangelist and teacher** pieces have been placed in their general area on the table; the **prophet** pieces have been taken out of the box and are being examined to determine where they go; the **apostle** pieces are just now beginning to be brought out of the box in the 1990's. So all systems and structures established before the year 2000 will be limited and temporary.

There will be much Reshuffling. In the current situation, it is as if all the ministries were dominoes, and we each have a hand of them that represents our revelation of fivefold ministry structure and function. The Holy Spirit will tell everyone to lay his or her own hand down so that He can transform them. Then we will all pick up the same hand so that we can then come forth with one revelation for structure rather than five. Consequently, we can expect a great deal of reshuffling and playing out those hands during the 90's.

Many ministers, and especially apostles, will come forth in the 90's to declare presumptuously that they have the perfect hand for playing out the role of fivefold ministry. But do not become bound or boxed in by one person's revelation. That person's hand of dominoes will have to be laid down and shuffled again before full and proper revelation comes in the beginning of the twenty-first century.

The Reshuffling Has Already Begun. Some ministers have already begun to establish guidelines and doctrines concerning proper structure and function for fivefold ministers. Many Pentecostal and Charismatic ministers are becoming nervous and concerned about the multitude of prophets that are arising. They do not know what to do with them and when, where and how to let them function, if at all. Some prophets are getting nervous and concerned about the restoration of apostles and are fearful that they will try to structure them into a restricted realm that God never intended.

This situation is creating the potential for some extreme teaching within the Prophetic and Apostolic Movements. I hope I can offer some understanding and encourage some balance in this area. The following chapter is devoted to bringing clarity to some of these potential controversies and extremes.

13

PROPHETS POSITIONS AND PRIVILEGES
AS ONE OF THE
FIVEFOLD MINISTERS

In the decade of the 1990's further illuminated understanding will come from the Holy Spirit to help fivefold ministers properly interrelate during the restoration of prophets and apostles. But, at the present, we are having to deal with statements and teachings that have been made by Church leaders that could hinder Christ's full purpose for His fivefold ministers.

Two Prideful Extremes to be Avoided. Already I am hearing from some quarters two teachings that are not biblically based and that unduly limit the function of ascension gift ministers. The first is *that only apostles can govern and be head administrators*. The second is *that only prophets can prophesy guidance, gifts and ministry.*

The seed bed from which these plants of extremism have sprouted is the alliterated list of one-word descriptions some have given for identifying the main ministry of each of the fivefold ministers. This list insists that **apostles govern, prophets guide, pastors guard, evangelists gather** and **teachers ground.** Because of these two words—"govern" for the apostle and "guide" for the prophet—the teaching has begun to be spread among certain circles of influential church leaders that prophets are not supposed to be in any headship ministry, such as pastor of a church, president of their own organization, or bishop/ overseer of an international fellowship of ministers.

I have diligently searched and can find no scriptures that put limitations on any of the fivefold ministers. There are no directives concerning when, where, how, or what some can or cannot minister. There are no biblical examples or scriptures which state that some of the fivefold ministers can hold certain positions in the Church and others cannot.

In Paul's writings to Timothy and Titus he gave directives concerning qualifications and standards for bishops, elders and deacons (1Tim.3:1-13; Titus 1:5-9). These are general instructions and requirements for those who will be in leadership within Christ's Church. But there are no statements in the New Testament that make a distinction between fivefold ministers in relation to qualifying standards of character or supernatural experiences, nor any distinctions or directives given concerning what positions can be held within the structure of the Church.

Five important insights must be considered and understood **concerning fivefold ministers**:

(1) They are all headship ministry, that is, they are an extension of the headship ministry of Jesus Christ, the Head of the Church. They are not "Body" ministries such as the gifts and ministries that the Holy Spirit gives to members of Christ's corporate Body. Technically speaking, they are not gifts of the Holy Spirit but ascension gifts of Jesus Christ Himself.

(2) All fivefold ministers are called to govern, guide, gather, ground and guard God's people. However, each has been given special grace and gifted ability in one of the areas more than the others. These one-word explanations should not be seen as limitations on each minister's activities, but rather as a one-word description of each one's major anointing and divinely-given ability.

(3) It is unscriptural and unwise to put an apostle, prophet, evangelist, pastor, or teacher into a box of limited anointings and activities. There are no scriptures which even suggest that fivefold ministers are limited to certain ministerial activities or leadership positions. The fivefold ascension gifts of Christ overlap and integrate just as the nine gifts of the Holy Spirit do.

Fivefold ministers are not independent ministries separated from one another but rather interdependent ministries vitally related to each other in Christ. They are the fivefold ministry of the one Christ. They are five parts of one whole. It takes all five working together to make the fullness of Christ's ministry to the Body of Christ. None are inferior or superior but all are anointed and appointed of God for a specific purpose.

(4) It is detrimental to the function of fivefold ministers for them to be categorized with details concerning personalities, performances and positions. The Holy Spirit is also grieved when people formulate methods for evaluating and determining a fivefold ministry office by some psychoanalysis technique or personality profile. God will not allow anything to take His place in this area.

(5) Each fivefold minister knows best his own calling and ministry. It is not the prerogative of the prophet to give guidelines, directions and restrictions on the ministry of the apostle. Likewise the apostle has not been granted authority from Father God to be daddy and director over the prophet. Only a prophet really knows the ministry and function of a prophet. And even one prophet should not try to box another prophet into his prophetic role, personality or performance. However we all must receive from one another and be subject to correction and adjustment in methodology and interrelationships.

Artificial Methods of Determining Ministry. Some ministers, teachers and theologians like to have every ministry organized and categorized in detail according to personality, performance and position. But such charts and designations cause those who teach them to put every ministry in a separate box. This may help some ministers to better understand their calling, but at the same time it will cause other ministers to think they are boxed in to those things designated on the chart for their area.

It may also cause novices to assume that they have a certian ascension gift and fivefold ministry calling simply because they seem to meet those descriptions. This results in determining a person's divine gifts or fivefold calling by some analysis chart instead of by a Holy Spirit revelation and conviction.

This is not to say that some forms of personality, skill, or interest analysis are not useful at all. Such tests and charts can be helpful in understanding individual temperaments, strengths and weaknesses. But that is not the same thing as identifying a person's divine **calling.**

Divine calling comes by Holy Spirit revelation. God sovereignly chooses to call whom He will for whichever purpose He will—and He often does so in spite of an individual's temperament, strengths, or weaknesses. The proof of that call is evidenced by a minister's submission to God's progressive training over a period of years. Afterwards the ministry is recognized by the rest of the Body of Christ because of the years of fruitful and consistent ministry—not by an analysis chart.

An Example of God's Sovereign Calling. We once had someone come to our campus to teach on knowing and recognizing ministry. He had researched some scientific medical studies on right and left brain functions. According to the results of the study, right brain people are more artistic, imaginative, intuitive and visionary. The left brain people are more analytical, mathematical, logical and practical.

All of this was useful information. But then the teacher went further to say that prophets would typically fit into the right brain group. So all of our prophets on the campus took the test to check his conclusion.

On a scale of 0-10, below 5 shows that the person functions more from the left brain and above five, the right brain. The teacher was shocked and puzzled to discover that all of our prophets except our prophetic worship leader scored below 5. My own score was 3.9, my wife's score was 5.0.

Whether these same results would hold for the majority of prophets is hard to say. But the point is that only one out of nine of our prophets who took the test scored as right brain people. The natural man wants to have a formula for everything rather than depend on the leading of the Spirit and revelation knowledge from Christ Jesus. But God will never allow us to come up with methods to take the place of Himself and the workings of His Holy Spirit.

Human-Made Analysis Charts Cannot Determine Divine Ministry. In all these prophetic pronouncements over me, confirmation of my calling to the ascension gift and ministry of prophet has been repeated over fifty times by numerous prophetic ministers through the years. I have also demonstrated more than thirty-eight years of proven, fruitful ministry as a prophet. But when I took the "motivational gifts" test, it concluded that my main motivational gifts were mercy and exhortation—not prophet.

Which should I believe—the prophecies which have gone over me and years of proven ministry, or some human-made chart for determining a person's gift? You cannot determine a divine God-ordained calling by some human analysis, even though it may use a few scriptures as a basis for its formulas and tests.

The motivational gifts test is good for insight into the human temperament a person was born with. Dividing people into "four temperaments" or testing them to determine motivational gifts or their unique human nature helps to understand why people act and react certain ways. It has other beneficial psychological benefits for understanding ourselves and counseling others. But none of those human-made systems can help a person determine his or her divine calling as a fivefold minister, or his or her membership ministry in the spiritual Body of Christ.

The divine seed of a spiritual gift or call must be planted by God, then incubated in the womb of prayer, obedience and spiritual growth until God's appointed time for birthing. After the ministry is birthed, then it must be nurtured, protected, exercised and progressively matured until all the person's potential reaches fullness of man or womanhood and ministry. There is a difference between the time of one's initial ministry calling and the time of one's full commissioning to that ministry position in the Body of Christ.

Human-Made Limitations vs. Abiding in Our Own Calling. Never swing to the extreme of limiting yourself or anyone else where Scripture does not impose a limitation or restriction. Only God knows the fullness of what He has called a person to be and become.

Nor should you swing to the other extreme of trying to be and do everything that other ministers are being and doing. Each calling and ministry has its own special purpose and performance. Be content in your calling while at the same time pressing toward the mark of apprehending all of that for which Christ has apprehended you (Phil.3:12-14; 1Cor.7:20).

The biblical principle concerning divine gifts and talents is that if you faithfully use what you have been given, then God will give you more (Mt.25:14-30). In fact, according to biblical principle, if you become a faithful and profitable servant, God will even take the talents from those unprofitable servants who are afraid to use what they have and give them to you to bless His Church (vv. 28-29). All things are possible to those who accept, believe and faithfully use what they have divinely received.

No One Person But Jesus Is All Five. Never allow your faith to become a presumptuous belief that you can have the calling and abilities of all fivefold ministers. Only Jesus had the fullness of all five ministries in one human body (Col.2:9). No other human can have the fullness of all five—not even the Pope, or an apostle over hundreds of ministers, or a pastor of a congregation of thousands.

Christ never did and never will give all five gifts and anointings to one person. But when He ascended on high He did give His ministry to men and women (Eph.4:8). He took His whole ministry mantle and distributed it into five parts, dividing

His wisdom, ability and performance into five categories. He designated them with certain titles that reveal these special gifts and ministries that He gave to his corporate Body. To some He gave His apostle mantle, to others His prophet ministry, to others His pastoral anointing, to others His evangelistic zeal and to still others His master teacher ability.

The Pastor Cannot Do It All Alone. I have seen some pastors who rarely have outside speakers in, as though they assume that they can perfect and properly equip the saints all by themselves. But there is no way a local congregation can reach proper biblical maturity and ministry without having mature ministry from the other fivefold ministers. There are no scriptures that even suggest that one senior shepherd of a local flock has been given all the truth and ministry needed to perfect his saints.

A pastor may conform his congregation to his doctrines, ways and ministries—but not into Christ's fullness. The Scriptures emphatically declare that it takes all five, including apostles, prophets, evangelists, pastors and teachers to do the job. All five are needed to perfect, mature and equip the saints for entering into the work of their membership ministries in the Body of Christ so that it is continually built up, "till we all come in the unity of the faith, and of the knowledge of the Son of God, unto a perfect man, unto the measure of the stature of the fullness of Christ" (Eph.4:13).

Same Ascension Gift, Different Performance. Not only does each of the five have their own unique calling and special gifting, but each of those called to the same office do not have the same personality, commission or performance. "Now there are diversities of gifts, but the same Spirit. And there are differences of administrations, but the same Lord. And there are diversities of operations, but it is the same God which worketh all in all" (1Cor.12:4-6). There are as many diversities of operations as there are people with ascension gifts.

Apostles Used As Examples of All. Of all the fivefold ministries, we have the most life examples of the apostle in the New Testament, with information relating to their calling, training and ministry. So we will use them to portray this truth which applies to all five.

Each of the original twelve apostles plus the thirteen others mentioned—including the apostle Paul—had their own particular calling and commission from the Lord Jesus Christ. God's different methods of calling and His special commissions for the Apostle Paul and the Apostle Peter demonstrate that people can have the same ascension gift while each nevertheless manifests a unique personality and performance.

Peter and Paul. Peter had no supernatural experience in his calling to be an apostle. He simply made his contact with Christ through his brother Andrew's effort to bring him to the Lord. After he had followed the Lord for awhile, Christ commissioned him as one of the twelve at the same time as the others.

Paul was not one of the original twelve, but came to know the Lord after Christ was resurrected and appeared to him in a supernatural blinding light on the road to Damascus. Paul's calling and commissioning came through this supernatural encounter with Jesus.

Peter had a limited education and no theological schooling. Paul was highly educated and probably had what would be equivalent today to a Doctor of Theology degree.

Peter was the first to receive the revelation while at Cornelius's house that Gentiles could become Christians without becoming proselyte Jews first. But it was Paul who received the commission from Christ to become the apostle to the Gentiles.

According to human logic it would seem that Paul should have been the apostle to the Jews and Peter the apostle to the Gentiles. But God does things His way, not ours. Apostle Peter was called and commissioned to be an apostle to the Jews but Paul received the commissioning from Christ to be an apostle to the Gentiles (2Tim. 1:11; Gal.2:7-9).

Both Peter and Paul were apostles. But each had a special

calling and commission from God, according to His sovereign choice.

Personality Profiles for Prophets. I was once asked, "After more than three decades as a prophet, can you give us the personality profile of a prophet?" I sought the Lord about it, and this was His answer:

"Take the twelve apostles and evaluate each of their personalities. If you can find that there is a consistent personality pattern for an apostle, then you can give a personality profile for prophets."

Needless to say, a study of the twelve apostles shows clearly that they were different in personality, natural motivation and character. There is no personality profile for apostles, prophets, evangelists, pastors, or teachers. There are no consistent human character traits that are unique to any one of the five.

I must say that I have noticed what seem to be some general traits in physical build, personality and mode of operation which seem to distinguish apostles and prophets. But I would not dare make them into a chart for analyzing and identifying someone's calling and ministry.

The original twelve apostles were privileged to walk and talk with Christ for over three years, but the other apostles mentioned were not. Only three of the twelve wrote material that became books in the Bible. Yet the Apostle Paul's writings produced fourteen New Testament books, more than that of all the twelve apostles together. For some of the apostles we have no record of their ever writing at all. (I am of course using the apostle as an example of standards and principles which apply to all fivefold ministers.)

Know Them by Their Fruit. The Bible offers no standards of personality, style of ministry, supernatural experiences, mode of ministry, or any formula by which we can classify some person as a fivefold minister. The only way a fivefold minister's calling can be determined is by a revelation from God; training for that ministry; and then the fruit of that ministry. Jesus does the calling and gifting, and He declares that it is by their fruit that you shall know them (Mt.7:16).

We can illustrate this further. Some are saying today that all apostles will be pastors of large successful churches and have several ministers and churches who look to them as their apostle-pastor. But the Apostle Paul during some thirty years of ministry never stayed as pastor of any one church for more than two or three years. He was mainly an itinerant minister who travelled all over the country as what we would call today an apostolic missionary. Paul won new converts to Christ and left them in the local synagogue or established a New Testament church with them. He returned to these churches on other ministry trips and established leadership in these congregations. He formed prophetic presbyteries and laid hands upon the candidates and prophesied to them their gifts and callings. Those he prophetically sensed had the calling and qualifications, he set in as the eldership ministry over that congregation (1Tim.4:14; 1:18; Acts 14:23).

In contrast, however, the Apostle James pastored the church in Jerusalem all the days of his ministry. As far as we know, he never travelled beyond his local area.

So anyone who forms a psychological chart or establishes standards of personality, positions and performances to determine whether someone is an apostle will do injustice to the callings and purposes of God for His fivefold ministers. It requires only a little thinking along this line to see that each minister is as unique in personality, power, performance, position and commission as five natural sons of one father would be different in these areas.

Can Prophets Govern and Be Heads of Ministry? If the one-word descriptions of the fivefold ministers' roles cited previously were allowed to become literal limitations (rather than suggestive descriptions), then **pastors** could **guard** the church but not be senior ministers in headship to **govern** the church. **Pastors** could **guard** the sheep but not **ground** them in the Word of God and church life, for that would have to be turned over to the

teachers. Apostles could **govern** but not until the prophets **guided** them in what to **govern** and how to **govern** it. We can thus easily see the unscriptural and impractical nature of such limiting notions of fivefold ministries.

One divine principle in biblical interpretation is that whatever was established in the Old Testament remains proper as a principle or practice unless the New Testament does away with it. For instance, tithing was established in the Old Testament, but since nothing is stated in the New that abolishes it, then it is still a proper practice for Christians. The same is true of worship and singing praises accompanied with all kinds of musical instruments, as was done in David's Tabernacle. And the same is also true concerning the ministry of the prophet.

Jesus came and fulfilled all things pertaining to the ceremonial law of sacrifices and offering. By the sacrifice of himself upon the cross he fulfilled the Old Covenant for humanity's relationship to God and established a New Covenant. In the New, Jesus is the only way for humankind to be forgiven of its sins and to have fellowship with God. For by one sacrifice He has made perfect forever those that are sanctified (He.10:14) and has become the end of the law for righteousness for all believers (Rom.10:4).

One God Who Does Not Change. Nevertheless, we do not serve one God of the Old Testament and another God of the New Testament. There is only one eternal God. He remains the same and shall never ever change. Jesus Christ is the same yesterday, today and forever (He.13:8). God the Father, Son, and Holy Spirit are One in nature, motivation and performance (Jn.5:7; Mk.12:29; Mal.3:6; Deut.4:35; Is.45:5; 47:8).

God has changed the ways for humanity to relate to Himself down through the ages and dispensations. But the God that has spoken through His prophets since the days of Adam is the same God that speaks through His prophets in the New Testament Church. The privileges, ministries and authority that the prophets had in the Old were not deleted in the New. Therefore, Old Testament prophets can properly be used as examples concerning what Church prophets can be and do (He.1:1; Lk.11:49; 1Cor.12:28).

Old Testament Prophets Prove That New Testament Prophets Can Govern. With these principles in mind we can now answer the question that has arisen in this movement concerning whether or not prophets can govern, administrate and be heads of ministries. We can find examples of prophets who founded a group of people, exercised senior headship, made final decisions for a great multitude and served as administrators of the material matters of a whole kingdom.

Abraham was a **prophet** (Gen.20:7) and he pioneered and fathered the Jewish people. He had the foundational ministry of establishing the borders of the land of Canaan. He received the revelation, call and commission from God for establishing the Jewish people. He was the head of hundreds of servants born and raised under his ministry. He was able to accumulate great wealth in material possessions.

Moses was a **prophet** (Acts 3:22; Hosea 12:13). He received divine revelation from God concerning His purpose for His people. He did not receive that divine guidance and then turn it over to an apostle to govern and administrate it. He demonstrated God's miraculous power and led over three million people out of bondage—then was senior pastor over them for forty years. He made the final decisions and administrated the affairs of God over His people.

Samuel was a **prophet** (1Sam.3:20). He did more than prophesy and give guidance. He was judge over the whole nation of Israel (1Sam.7:15-17). He founded the schools of the prophets and established them in cities throughout Israel. He had his home and headquarters in Ramah but travelled throughout the nation. He was head of his own ministerial association. He anointed and ordained other prophets to the ministry. He also ordained priests, Levites, porters and two kings over all Israel. (1Chr.9:22; 1Sam.9:16,17; 10:1). He was bishop-overseer of the company of prophets that he established during his day (1Sam.19:20).

David was a **prophet** (Acts 2:29,30) and he was king and administrator of all the affairs of the nation of Israel. Both Prophet Moses and Prophet David received revelation knowledge for the building of God's house. Moses received the pattern for the Tabernacle and David received the blueprint for the Temple that Solomon built (1Chr.28:11,12). **Joseph** was probably a **prophet,** for he had dreams, interpreted dreams and eventually was made overseer of all the nation of Egypt. **Daniel** was a **prophet** (Mt.24:15) who received and interpreted many dreams. He was made president and overseer of all the princes in the great Babylonian Empire.

Jesus Christ was a **prophet** (Lk.24:19; Acts 3:22,23; Jn.4:19,44; 6:14; 7:40; 9:17) and He established the New Testament Church. He continues to give headship directives and to administer the affairs of the Church. Jesus was the first New Testament Church prophet, and He set the pattern for all of His Church prophets.

These examples of just a few biblical prophets should be sufficient to show that God has invested much more ability within His prophets than just enough to make them a mouth piece for guidance. We will not take space to speak in detail of other prophets and prophetesses that had similar responsibilities such as Isaiah, Deborah and others.

Apostles and Prophets the Foundation. In the New Testament Church Paul declares that prophets along with the apostles are foundational ministries upon which the Church is built: "You are built upon the foundation of the apostles and prophets, Jesus Christ himself being the Chief Corner Stone" (Eph.2:20). Nowhere in Scripture does it say that the apostle has any more wisdom or authority from Christ for building churches on a proper foundation than the prophet.

God's true apostles and prophets are not in competition with each other. They were designed by Christ to complement each other. They are the only two of the five that are paired together in ministry and that have similar anointed abilities. Paul declares that they are the two fivefold ministers who have the anointing to receive revelation from Christ concerning the new truths that God wants to bring forth: "by revelation He made known unto me the mystery...when ye read, ye may understand my knowledge in the mystery of Christ which in other ages was not made known unto the sons of men, as it is now revealed unto his holy **apostles** and **prophets** by the Spirit" (Eph.3:3-5).

Apostles and prophets were the first two ministries that God set in the Church: "And God hath set some in the church, first **apostles**, secondarily **prophets**" (1Cor. 12:28). They are the two ministries sent by Jesus who He said would be persecuted and rejected the most by the old religious order: "I will send them **prophets** and **apostles**, and some of them they shall slay and persecute" (Lk.11:49). In fact, it is shedding the blood of the prophets that brings the wrath of God upon the Babylonian harlot system described in Revelation: "And in her was found the blood of **prophets**, and of saints" (Rev. 18:24).

Prophets and apostles are thus co-laboring ministries with a kindred spirit that will be alive and functioning as long as mortal human beings are alive on planet earth.

Apostles Can Prophesy Guidance, Gifts and Ministries. Just as prophets can govern and be heads of ministry, the Bible records that apostles can prophesy guidance, gifts and ministries. The Apostle Paul laid hands upon Timothy and prophesied his gifts and ministry (1Tim.4:14). And he longed to see the Roman Christians that he might lay hands on them and impart to them some spiritual gifts (Rom.1:11).

The Apostle Paul and the Prophet Silas co-labored equally together in establishing the first New Testament Church in Ephesus. Even so, present-day apostles and prophets must be diligent to keep out the divisive teaching and extreme statements that limit, or any practices that would hinder, the close working relationship between prophets and apostles.

Apostolic-Prophets and Prophetic-Apostles. Some people called to be a prophet have progressed and matured in manhood and ministry over many years. The fruit of their years of ministry has proven that they have been commissioned by Christ to fulfill a senior leadership and fatherhood ministry to other leaders in the Body of Christ. They are prophets to whom many other fivefold ministers look as a prophetic father in the faith. Such prophets have become what I call an **apostolic-prophet**.

Others are called to the ascension gift of apostle and also to fulfill a greater role of leading and directing others in the Body of Christ. They have matured in manhood and ministry over several decades until many other ministers begin to look to them for fatherhood covering, relationship and accountability. They have exercised their spiritual senses, sharpened their prophetic perspective and developed their apostolic revelation anointing. They are not depending on their own organizational ability, wisdom, or senior leadership position, but are exercising their revelation anointing plus the supernatural signs and wonders ministry of an apostle. This type of apostle is what I believe to be a **prophetic-apostle**.

In the Church today certain men of God are alive who are truly prophetic and apostolic fathers of the faith. It is these true apostolic-prophets and prophetic-apostles whom God wants to use to establish His restorational movements being brought forth in the 80's and 90's.

Same Calling, But Not the Same Capability. All who are called to the office of prophet do not have the same commission to fulfill in the Body of Christ. Some are local church prophets whom God has not enabled to pastor a church, head up their own ministry, or write books. Some are called as Agabus was just to give the word of the Lord to key people now and then. Some are called like Daniel to be in the business world and will never have a pulpit position.

The Scripture establishes no precedent declaring that a person must have a pulpit position to be a fivefold minister. (I personally believe, however, that all fivefold should be ordained ministers). If having your own **pulpit** was necessary evidence of the calling to a fivefold ministry, then the only ministers called to fivefold offices would be senior pastors of their own churches.

Everyone called to be an apostle is not given the commission to be a head over other ministers, the senior pastor of a large church, or to pioneer into unevangelized areas for establishing new churches. This is important to remember when someone receives a prophecy of a calling to the prophetic or apostolic office.

Prophesying Fivefold Callings Can Cause Confusion. Problems sometimes arise when prophets, or those who participate in prophetic presbytery teams, prophesy a fivefold ministry calling to a person. When the person's experience does not seem to match up with the prophecy, the problem may lie in one of several areas. Sometimes those prophesying may be missing God. But the majority of the time it is the improper response of the one receiving the prophecy that creates the confusion. This is especially true when the calling of apostle or prophet is prophesied.

Often people receiving the prophetic word may have a wrong concept of the ministry prophesied. They may immediately try to enter into that ministry and fulfill it before God's timing. They may not understand the process and years of preparatory experiences God takes people through before commissioning them to that ascension gift calling. So anyone who has received a divine calling of apostle or prophet should not immediately make name cards with apostle or prophet titles, no more than one who receives the calling of pastor should take on that title until he or she is officially functioning in that capacity.

Modern Day Apostolic-Prophets and Prophetic-Apostles. Some Christian teachers and theologians have described the ministry of an apostle as being that of an administrator and spiritual overseer of ministers and churches—similar to the ministry of a pastor as the overseer of church members, deacons and other leadership ministries within the local church. We can better evaluate this idea if we provide a historical context for the office of overseer in the Church.

The Historical Development of "Bishop". After an initial three hundred years of rejection and persecution by Judaism and the nations of the world, Christianity became an accepted religion within the Roman Empire. This change was made law by the Roman emperor Constantine, who issued an "Edict of Toleration" in A.D. 313 allowing Christianity to function publicly the same as any other religion or secular society. Christian churches moved from being underground to government-recognized. Christians were allowed citizenship and the right to hold political offices. Within a few years hundreds of churches were built throughout the Roman Empire and other parts of the world. Local congregations began to relate to certain translocal leaders, and the leaders began to press for position and control.

Centralization of Control. At the close of the Apostolic Age, churches were independent of each other, shepherded by fivefold ministers who were generally called pastors or elders. The main leader or senior pastor came to be called "bishop," which means "overseer." Gradually, the jurisdiction of the bishop came to include neighboring churches in other towns.

Bishop Calixtus (a bishop of Rome A.D. 217-222) was the first to base his claim to authority on Matthew 16:18. The great theologian Tertullian of Carthage called Calixtus a usurper in speaking as if he were the "Bishop of Bishops." When Constantine called the council of Nicea in A.D. 325 and presided over the first worldwide council of churches, he accorded the bishops of Alexandria and Antioch full jurisdiction over their provinces, as the Roman Bishop had over his.

By the end of the fourth century the eastern bishops had come to be called "patriarchs." They were of equal authority, each having full control of his own province. The five bishops/patriarchs who dominated Christendom at the time were headquartered in Rome, Constantinople, Antioch, Jerusalem and Alexandria. After the division of the Roman Empire into East and West, the struggle for the leadership of Christendom was between Rome (Roman Catholics) and Constantinople (Eastern Orthodox).

Development of the One-Man Rule Papal Religious Structure.
In the earlier centuries of the Church the bishops came to be
affectionately addressed as "Papa" (Father), which gave rise to
the word "Pope." About the year A.D. 500, "Papa" began to be
restricted in its use by the local bishops, and the title was
eventually reserved exclusively for the bishop of Rome.

Over the centuries the word came to mean "Universal
Bishop." The idea that the bishop of Rome should have authority
over the whole Church grew slowly and was bitterly contested.
By the middle of the Dark Ages the papal reign of one-man rule
had reached a position of supreme power and international
jurisdiction.

Prophets and Apostles Both Needed. Religious people have a
way of taking what is scriptural, sacred and workable and
converting it into a lifeless religious form which restricts God's
purpose and brings bondage to His people. When the Church
becomes more structural than spiritual, it becomes petrified
wood instead of a fruitful growing tree. When it becomes more
spiritual than structural, it becomes dissipating and destructive
flood waters without any control or order.

For this reason, both apostles and prophets must be prominent and co-equal in laying the foundation for the Church. No
church will have a balanced and proper foundation and function
without the ministry of both apostles and prophets.

If a church is built with the ministry of the apostle alone,
without the prophet ministry, then it becomes so structured and
ordered that it becomes lifeless and formal without the fiery
flow of praise and power. If it is built by the prophet alone,
without the ministry of the apostle, the people become so spiritually activated that everyone is a law unto him or herself, and it
leads to fanaticism. But with the ministry of both the apostle and
prophet the Church of Jesus Christ will maintain a balance
between structure and spirituality, doctrine and demonstration,
prophetic perspective and spirituality and apostolic order and
authority.

Who Can Be a Bishop? The word **bishop** is a scriptural term (1Tim.3:1; Titus 1:7; 1Pet.2:25). It can rightly be used as a title that designates a fivefold minister who oversees other people and ministries. The bishop may be the senior pastor of a local church, or the apostolic-prophet or prophetic-apostle over several ministers and churches. It is not necessarily a fivefold calling but an administrative office which is given by others and not by oneself.

The use of the title "bishop" is not wrong if the person bearing the title meets its qualifications, and if the motive and purpose for its usage are according to biblical principles. But if the office of bishop develops into a pyramid papal system as it did during the deterioration of the Church, then it becomes wrong.

The International Communion of Charismatic Churches. A group of present-truth church leaders have had bestowed upon them the title of "bishop" and are seeking to use it in its proper biblical context. They are not building a pyramid system or trying to divide the church world up into their oversight. But they are each head of their own group of ministers and churches without any legal or organizational responsibility to each other. This association reflects a spiritual commitment and a coming together for mutual relationship and accountability within the Body of Christ. Thousands of churches and ministers across several continents of the world are represented by these bishops. They recognize that all fivefold ministers are capable of maturing to the place of becoming prophetic or apostolic ministers.

This group chose the name International Communion of Charismatic Churches (ICCC) for their identification. Each year one of the bishops is appointed by the rest to chair the meetings when they come together. They usually meet once or twice a year.

For them, the title of "bishop" shows their desire to serve and be responsible for those who are looking to them for spiritual oversight. To be invited to become one of the bishops a person must have demonstrated proof of ministry and oversight ability by years of fruitful fatherhood ministry that has caused hundreds of ministers and churches to be drawn to him and established by him.

My Invitation to Join the ICCC. In 1987 the chairman of the ICCC bishops gave me an invitation to become one of their number. I met with them in Atlanta, and after full evaluation and prayerful consideration they were in unanimous agreement for me becoming a bishop among them.

In addition to the leading of the Holy Spirit and my proven ministry as an apostolic-prophet, president and overseer of the Christian International Network of Prophetic Ministries, there was one unique reason for their decision. The presiding bishop, Earl Paulk, stated at the formal consecration service that one reason they desired for me to become a bishop among them was that they had every fivefold ministry represented among their bishops except that of a mature proven prophet with international recognition of that office.

Bishop Earl Paulk (of Chapel Hill Harvester Church, Atlanta, GA) and Bishop John Meares (of Evangel Temple, Washington, D.C.) came as representatives of the ICCC to the January 1989 meeting of the CI-NPM ministers in Destin, Florida. They called forth certain of our ministers to represent different areas of our ministry. Pastor Tom Hamon stood representing the local church. Evelyn Hamon stood with the rest for the laying on of hands to represent the family. Dr. Randy Adler stood for the CI-NPM Board of Governors; Prophet Eddie Traut represented the prophetic ministers from overseas; and Pastor-Prophet Jim Davis stood representing the body of NPM ministers and members.

The whole purpose of this history is to show that there are national church leaders who recognize the principle that "fathers of the faith" can come forth from among all fivefold ministers.

Every leader needs a relationship of mutual accountability with peers and seniors outside of those who are under his immediate oversight. There is no rank among the fivefold, only a commissioning to a place of greater servanthood and responsibility within the Body of Christ. The divine right to be the head of a ministry is not based on a person's fivefold calling, but rather upon years of faithfulness to mature in manhood and ministry. Our calling is based on God's sovereignty, but our commissioning includes our responsibility to respond properly in obedience to become purified and matured in motive and manhood with a continuing, productive ministry.

The bishops in the ICCC recognize that **prophets** can administrate and take the spiritual oversight of ministers and churches. In this day and hour, among those ministers who are called to the two foundational ministries of prophet and apostle, Jesus Christ is commissioning some to be **apostolic-prophets** and **prophetic-apostles.**

14

THE DIVINE PROCESS
IN PROPHETIC FULFILLMENT

In Ezekiel 37:1-14 we read that the prophet Ezekiel was taken by the hand of God and brought by the Spirit to a valley of many dry bones. The Lord had him walk among the multitude of human bones in the valley. Then God asked Ezekiel if he thought these bones could come together and live. He responded by declaring that only God knew the answer to that question. So God told the prophet that they could and would live if he would prophesy to that valley of dry bones.

Those bones represented the whole house of Israel, God's chosen people who had backslidden away from God and were dry and scattered. God declared that the prophesying of the prophet would be the key that would bring life, restoration and activation of God's people into the army of the Lord. However, this would not happen at once; it will require a process that takes place step by step (Deut.7:22).

This is what we call the **prophetic process**, and it follows the same pattern whether it is prophecy coming forth to the world, to a nation, to a church or to an individual. According to this scriptural passage, eight progressive steps must take place:

(1) Noise. The noise came from two sources. First was the thundering voice of prophecy as expressed in Psalm 29, where the "voice of the Lord" is repeated seven times, describing what His voice is and what it does.

The second was the noise of all those bones coming together. Can you imagine millions of bones suddenly arising at the commanding voice of prophecy, flying about and bumping against each other as they sought to find their proper place in a human skeleton?

The first thing that happens in the prophetic process is the sound of the prophecy being spoken. As people and things begin to respond to that word, as much confusion and jostling about takes place as when the bones arose and started coming together. We hear the progressive noisy voices of confusion, concern and then finally clarity. The first sign of a creative prophecy is not necessarily peace and harmony, but noise and confusion. But if everyone holds steady in faith, then clarity with a clear prophetic direction comes forth.

(2) Shaking. The second thing that happens in the prophetic process is a great shaking. I have never seen it fail yet that after a person receives a prophetic word, that person goes through a great shaking in his or her life. The Prophetic Movement was birthed in 1988, and there was much prophesying to the nations of the world taking place in the 80's. The result was a great shaking in all realms like an earthquake (He.12:27; Is.40:4; Hag.2:6,7,21,22).

The Berlin wall was shaken down and the Iron Curtain was ripped apart. Dictators came tumbling down in countries like Panama. Religious leaders who had immorality in their lives were shaken loose from their international popularity.

In God's commission to Jeremiah as a prophet (Jer. 1:10), we read that his prophecies had to do twice as much shaking, tearing down, rooting out and destroying the roots and rubble before there could be planting and building. It is like clearing land for farming or preparing ground for laying the foundation of a building. When a true prophet with a pure prophetic word comes to a church or an individual, that word is apt to cause a great shaking to take place before the remaining five steps are fulfilled.

It is like the word of the Lord that came through Gideon to Israel concerning victory over their enemies. It rooted out and shook the 31,700 men who had responded to the trumpet call before it brought the 300 together in unity to win the battle. Like Moses going back to Egypt to fulfill that glorious prophecy of the Exodus of Israel, things got worse before the prophecy began to work (Jdg.6:1-8:35; Ex.5:1-23)

A divine principle in the prophetic process is that it nearly always gets worse before it gets better. If you have received a major prophecy concerning great growth in your church or great ministry, deliverance or prosperity for your life—yet everything seems to be doing the opposite by falling apart and getting worse—then rejoice, for you are in stage two of the prophetic process. Hold steady in faith and you will progress on to stage three (Heb.10:35,36; 12:1-3,25-28; Gal.6:9).

(3) Coming Together. After the Lord has taken care of everything He wants shaken down and destroyed, and proper adjustments have been made, then begins the time when plans, people and provisions begin to come together. There is nothing greater than when a prophetic plan comes together and the people and provisions are provided for its fulfillment.

The Prophetic Movement will be noised abroad, which will cause a great shaking in the religious world. But then those who are called to walk on in restored truth will come together, bone to bone. They will be a skeleton group, but not forever—God has four more progressive steps in His prophetic process of bringing a divine purpose to pass.

(4) Muscle and Flesh. After the skeleton of the prophetic purpose has come together, the things that will give strength and a well-rounded ministry are needed. So God puts sinews and flesh on the body to give strength, fullness and divine enablement. After a movement is birthed, has gone through its shaking and has had a coming together of the people, then the prophetic process brings structure, order, wisdom and anointing for holding it together and directing the movement of the skeleton with power and wisdom. This does not mean the creation of human-made organizations, but rather divine guidelines, structure and relationships that help people both inside and outside of the movement to relate together.

In an individual's life, prophetic process step number four is when God gives the divine enablement and wisdom to act upon the prophetic word and to put muscle and fullness into the prophetic promise.

(5) Skin. This is the covering placed over the body to protect it from the negative elements it encounters. When a human body is covered with second and third-degree burns, it cannot hold the proper fluids in nor can it protect itself from the invasion of germs from without. A person with that kind of burns must be isolated in a germ-free room or wrapped with an artificial covering.

Many of us have been spiritually burned in life—some of us even have "third-degree" spiritual burns. This causes us not to be able to hold the Body of Christ fluids of peace and joy, and it leaves us with no protection against the germs of discouragement and disease unless we allow someone else to help us.

In the prophetic process the skin stage represents several areas. You need to keep your family relationship as a covering and protection. You must maintain local church membership and pastoral covering. If you are a senior minister of your own ministry, then you need covering by a national fellowship of ministers with a present-truth apostolic-prophet or prophetic-apostle at the head of it.

Spiritually, the skin covering is the garment of praise and a positive forgiving attitude toward all who have trespassed against us. Skin represents the thing that enables us to adjust to varying circumstances of life. Our skin helps the body adapt to hot and cold atmospheres.

We must develop a thick skin and tough hide if we are going to make it in this day and hour. Thin-skinned people will not make it, to say nothing of those who have not allowed any skin to be placed over them. Especially prophets and prophetic people must not be easily offended. They will never maintain their ministries if they have a spirit of rejection, persecution complex, unforgiving attitude, or a vengeful response to pressure and persecution. God is raising up an army in this prophetic process, so we all must learn to "endure hardship as a good soldier of Jesus Christ" (2Tim.2:3).

(6) Breath of Life. When God brought forth His prophetic purpose of "let us make man," He first shook the earth, picked up a handful of clay, and built a bone structure. Then He placed sinew and flesh upon that skeleton and covered it with skin. Finally God took that body of man and breathed into it the breath of life, and man became a living soul.

Ezekiel's first prophesying caused the first five steps of the prophetic process to take place. But he had to prophesy again to bring life within the body.

In the process of restoration, John Huss and Martin Luther prophesied and prophetically preached until it shook the religious kingdoms of that day and hour and brought forth the beginning of the great restoration period of the Church. Each movement thereafter has brought the Church, the corporate Body of Christ, through the different stages to its present status.

The Prophetic Movement and Apostolic Movement are designed to be a new prophetic voice to the Body of Christ until resurrection life flows into the Church and it stands up and starts marching throughout the earth as the great army of the Lord. This prophetic movement is to prophesy life to the Body of Christ.

The last generation of the mortal Church will have a greater supernatural resurrection life and power. A special glory, salvation, power and demonstration has been prophetically predestined for the last generation of the mortal Church. God declares, " Behold, I will do a new thing," and we are to look for that great salvation ready to be revealed in these last days. Before Christ's literal and personal second coming there will be a coming of Christ in revelation knowledge to bring the Church to fullness of truth and maturity (Is.43:19; He.9:28; 2Pet. 1:7-13).

(7) Army of the Lord. The end result of the prophesying of the prophet Ezekiel was that the scattered valley of dry bones was brought together with muscle, flesh and then the breath of life to become an exceedingly great army, activated into warfare ministry. God's purpose for the company of prophets' being brought forth is to continue prophesying until the Church arises as a great army of Godly soldiers.

Chapters 6 through 9 (pages 365-387) in *The Eternal Church* give all the relevant scriptures and a description of the army of the Lord executing God's judgments in the last move of God within and through the Church. The Church has always been an army, but it is being prepared to fight the final battle under the headship of its Commander-in-Chief, Jesus Christ.

Co-Laborers Together Forever. Jesus Christ purchased His Church to be His co-laborer, His united Bride, one with Him in all that He is and shall ever be or shall ever do. Everything that Jesus shall ever do again from now to eternity will be done in, through, and with His Church. He will never do anything ever again without His Church-Bride being a part with Him in its fulfillment. He has delegated His power of attorney to His Church for the performance of His eternal purpose. All things yet to be revealed, restored, or fulfilled will be accomplished in, by and through His Church. (See *The Eternal Church*, page 368.)

In every scripture in the Bible speaking of Christ's subduing all His enemies, the Church is intimately joined with Him in that co-laboring ministry (1Cor.6:2,3; Rom.8:17-19; Jn.14:12; 17:18; Is.54:17; Song.S.6:10,13; Joel 2:1-12; Ps.91; Rev.6:2; cf. Rom.8:37; Ps.149:6-9; Jude 1:15; Rev.1:5,6; 2:26,27; 3:21; 5:9,10; 19:11-16; 20:4,6.)

(8) Restoration to Home Land: Saints Take the Kingdom. The final result for Israel in this prophetic process was that they were to take back their home land that had belonged prophetically to their father Abraham. The final result of the prophetic process within God's people, the Church, is that they will take back their home land that belongs to their Father God.

Planet earth belongs to God and the righteous, not to the

devil and the wicked (Ps.24:1; 50:6; 1Cor.10:26). Revelation 10:7 declares that when the prophets begin to echo on earth in prophecy the trumpet sound of the message of the seventh angel in heaven, all the mysteries of God will finally be revealed and made known to the Church. Fullness of truth brings fullness of life, anointing and power to produce and fully possess our promised possessions.

This happens in the "days" of the voice of the seventh angel and the prophesying of the prophets. The end result of the seventh angel's sounding of his trumpet in heaven and the prophets' prophesying on earth is the divine declaration that "the kingdoms of this world are become the kingdoms of our Lord, and of his Christ; and he shall reign for ever and ever" (Rev.11:15).

Please take note that in all this prophetic process, prophecy plays a vital role in activating the bones and bringing them together in structure and strength. Prophecy brings life into the body and causes it to rise up as an exceedingly great army. The army of the Lord is activated by prophecy into warfare and does not cease its ministry until it subdues all the enemies of Christ and lays them at His feet, where He provisionally ordained them to be when He rose from the dead.

Prophecy that is truly divinely ordained is God speaking. God is the Creator, and when He speaks, things are created and brought into existence which did not exist before He spoke. (God prophetically spoke all natural creation into existence; Genesis 1-2.) Prophecy activates the predestinated purposes of God to come forth in His timing. Prophets are to know the secret times and seasons of God.

Prophecy is the germinating, activating power that brings forth ministry the same as water sprouts seeds which have been lying dormant in dry ground. Anointed personal prophecy to a person by a mature prophet or prophetic presbytery activates divinely predestined ministry which has been lying dormant within the Church member or Christian minister. True prophecy is powerful and penetrates to the depth of the heart-soil it enters. The quality of soil determines the type of plant that can be produced from the prophetic word-seed. Those who want to derive the most from the prophets and prophetic ministry must allow God to break up their fallow ground and take the weed seeds out so that their prophetic word can come to full maturity and ministry. Believe God and be established. Receive and believe His prophets and prosper (Hosea 10:12; 2Chr.20:20; Amos 3:7; Eph.3:5; Mt.13:3-9,18-23).

15

PROPHETIC CONCLUSION AND CHARGE

After reading this book you should have concluded from scriptural examples that God has prophets being voices for Him from Genesis to Revelation, in every dispensation and age throughout the history of the human race. The scriptures emphatically declare that Christ gave prophets along with evangelists, pastors, teachers and apostles to be an extension of His continuing personal ministry to His Church.

Jesus gave the fivefold ministry to minister to the saints for their equipping and maturing so that they could enter into the work of their membership ministry in the living corporate Body of Christ. The ascension gifted fivefold ministers are to continue ministering throughout the Church Age until the universal Church of Jesus Christ comes into "the unity of the faith, and of the knowledge of the Son of God, unto a perfect man, unto the measure of the stature of the fullness of Christ" (Eph.4:13).

Prophets and apostles are a permanent and continuing ministry within the Church just as evangelists, pastors and teachers are. Protestants reacting to the erroneous teaching of apostolic succession counteracted with the presumptuous teaching that Christ withdrew the ministry of apostles after the Church was founded and the Bible written. The fundamentalists dispensationally depleted the ministry of the prophet to discredit the claims of Mormonism and other cultic groups such as Islam; these groups had claimed that their leaders were prophets and had received visions and revelations resulting in the Book of Mormon and the Koran, which are considered by their followers to have the same authority as the Bible.

But two wrongs do not make a right. The answer is not to do away with the office of apostle and prophet, but rather to allow the Holy Spirit and the Logos Word of God to give us proper understanding of their place and function within the Body of Christ.

Timely and Divinely Directed. The Prophetic Movement is a truly God-ordained, Jesus-designed and Holy Spirit-directed movement. Like all past Holy Spirit movements, it is bringing enlightened understanding, activation and re-establishment of certain vital truths and ministries within the Church. The Church is destined to come to the fullness of truth with the full knowledge and manhood of Christ Jesus, and the Prophetic Movement is one more giant step in that divine destiny.

Each person who becomes exposed to the movement will have opportunity to receive it or reject it. Those who do receive will be in three categories. The thirtyfold group will only perceive and receive; the sixtyfold group will propagate and portray; and then the hundredfold group will not only do what the other two groups have done, but will also publish and practice prophetic ministry until they produce a great army of God's prophetic people.

Those who reject will also be three groups—the passive; the perturbed; and those past movement religious leaders who persecute purposefully.

There is a Restorational Prophetic Movement. The Holy Spirit is continuing His commissioned task of bringing the Church into all truth and restoring within the Church all that was once actively there. The Prophetic Movement is ordained of God and headed by Christ Jesus for the bringing forth of His great company of prophets. The Prophetic Movement has a specific purpose to accomplish, as did each restoration movement that has taken place during the last five hundred years of Church restoration.

The Prophetic Movement is preparing the way for the Apostolic Movement, which will finalize the full restoration and activation of all fivefold ascension gift ministers.

No Competition in the Body of Christ. The true prophets and apostles will not be in competition with each other, but will be a complement to each other in Christ Jesus. The prophets and apostles have the responsibility of preparing the way and making ready a people for the second coming of Christ. They will minister in the power and spirit of Elijah in fulfillment of the prophet Malachi's words (Mal.4:5,6).

One prophet, John the Baptist, fulfilled that prophecy concerning the first coming of Christ, but a company of prophets will fulfill that prophecy concerning the second coming of Christ. Anyone who hinders the work of the Holy Spirit in fulfilling the purpose of Christ for His Church prophets will be in serious trouble with God. God's purpose for the Prophetic Movement is dear and meaningful to Christ.

Jesus Wants to Return Soon! Jesus deeply desires to return for His Church and to see all wickedness removed from His earth. For the earth is the Lord's and the fullness thereof. He earnestly longs for the day when all enemies of righteousness are cast into the lake of fire and His Church and planet earth are conformed to His image and purpose with Him as King of kings and Lord of lords.

The true prophets being activated today are ordained to play a vital role in bringing that divine purpose into reality. This is a serious matter to Jesus, and He will deal severely with anyone who hinders those who are making the proper preparation for His soon return. His eternal decrees still stands today: "Touch not my anointed and do my prophets no harm" and "Despise not prophesying."

Prophetic Charge for Unity. My prophetic perception and personal belief is that Christ is not going to tolerate among His prophets the petty party spirit that prevailed among past movement leaders. The devil will seek to divide and devour by setting one prophetic camp against another. He will try to magnify the differences in the Prophetic Movement leaders' perception of prophets and prophetic ministry.

My fellow Prophetic Movement leaders, we must, for Christ's sake and purpose, work together in unity. We may not all agree on particular points, but we all do agree that there are prophets in the Church today. There is no one major prophet or a dozen prophetic leaders that we all must be submitted to, but we all need to relate in the spirit of cooperation and unity for the restoration of Christ's prophets.

Let us not allow different convictions, experiences and manifestations to keep us from accepting each other as Church prophets. Some of us may say that prophecy only confirms and others of us may say that prophets will speak new things to people. Some may be convinced that a person must have certain spiritual experiences—out-of-body experiences, visions of Jesus, or angelic visitations—as proof of call to the office of prophet. Others may not have those experiences or convictions, but are equally called and effective as prophets.

We must make allowance for each other's convictions and experiences. Fellow prophets, other religious leaders will seek to box us into their limited understanding and theology concerning prophets, but please let us not be caught up in that web of the devil's tactic to restrict and hinder the prophets from being one united company of prophets fulfilling Christ's purpose. If the Scriptures do not put a limitation or restriction in that area of prophetic ministry, then let us not impose one.

No one prophetic camp or group will have all the truth, all the proper practices and all the proper ways of administering prophetic ministry.

An Appeal to the Apostles. I make an earnest appeal to those called and commissioned to the office of apostle not to be critical and condemning, but to be companions with the prophets. We are determined to stand with you in your day of full restoration within the Church.

I have personally surrounded myself with prophetic-apostles and apostolic-prophets to provide balance and proper structure while maintaining the prophetic flow and freedom to grow and mature in manhood and ministry. I believe I have as much concern and as great a burden for balance, integrity and purity of ministry and manifestations with proper structure as any apostle I know. We prophets have the most to lose if proper balance is not maintained and biblical principles are not practiced.

I believe I speak for most of the Prophetic Movement leaders when I say that we are open to dialogue to find the ways of wisdom in fulfilling this divine commission from Christ. I am open for correction and instruction in wisdom for ways and means that are more profitable in propagating the prophetic. But if you start asking me to deny my convictions and commission from Christ, then I would have to take the same stand that Martin Luther took at the Diet of Worms when the religious hierarchy demanded that he recant and renounce all of his teachings and books.

Present-truth apostles and prophets will work together in cooperation with Christ to fulfill His purpose. But the old wine-skin movement apostles, pastors and denominational hierarchy who do not accept the truth that there are Church prophets today will make declarations against this movement and write books to discredit its divine validity.

Everyone Will Respond. According to five hundred years of Church History Movements, the present-day leaders of the last move of God always become some of the main persecutors of the present-day move of God. This then means that present-day church leaders whose church or ministry was established during movements such as the Latter Rain, Charismatic, Faith or Kingdom movements will respond one of three ways: They will become persecutors, they will be passively indifferent, or they will participate. Those who want to participate but are in the classical Pentecostal denominations that reject the restoration of apostles and prophets may have to come out to come into the fullness of the Prophetic Movement truths.

Those churches which have been established from the last four movements after the Pentecostal Movements believe and practice the sovereign headship of the local pastor and believe each local church should be indigenous. This means that the pastor does not have to leave or change anything, but simply incorporate these truths and spiritual blessings into his local ministry.

The Prophetic Movement is not designed by God to be an island to itself or to gather everyone to its banner. It is of God and is designed to be activated in every part of Christendom where they will allow the recognition and ministry of apostles, prophets and prophetic ministry, with all of its blessings and practices. I believe there are apostles and prophets in every denomination and Christian group where there are born-again and Spirit-filled men and women of God. But they may not recognize them by that name or allow them to function in their true biblical apostolic and prophetic ministry.

I pray that those who have the divine calling to be prophets will come in contact with this book and be encouraged and enlightened to become all that God wants them to be. Those whom God has called to be apostles and prophets and to walk in present truth will witness in their spirit to this truth and allow the Holy Spirit to activate them into fulfilling their true ordained calling. The Church members who read this book and have the Joshua generation spirit will arise to become God's prophetic people in this day and hour, demonstrating the supernatural gifts of the Holy Spirit.

Response to the Prophets Is Critical. Christians must recognize the seriousness of accepting or rejecting God's prophets. It has always been true—and in this Prophetic Movement will be especially true—that the way we respond to God's divinely-established prophets will determine our success or failure, life or death, captivity or freedom. Whole nations have arisen or fallen based on their response to God's word through His prophets.

Even God's chosen nation of Israel lost their liberty and went into captivity because of their wrong attitude and response to God's prophets:

And the Lord, the God of their fathers, sent to them persistently by His messengers [**prophets**], because He had compassion on His people and on His dwelling place. But they kept mocking the messengers of God and despising His words and scoffing at **His prophets** till the wrath of the Lord rose against His people, till there was no remedy or healing. Therefore He brought against them the king of the Chaldeans... (2Chr.36: 15-16).

The biblical writer then goes on to describe the bondage and horrible sufferings of the Israelites, and how they were carried away to Babylon to remain in captivity for seventy years. This not only happened because of their response to God's prophet messengers but "to fulfill the Lord's word by the prophet Jeremiah" (see vv.16-21)

The destiny of individuals, churches, denominations, businesses, nations and world empires rise or fall according to the word of the Lord. And most of His personal words spoken concerning specific people and places come through His prophets. So Jehoshaphat's admonition to his people applies to all people today: "Believe in the Lord your God, so shall you be established; believe his prophets, so shall you prosper" (2Chr. 20:20).

Jesus declared that "he that receives a prophet in the name of a prophet shall receive a prophet's reward" (Mt.10:41). God gives great blessings and rewards to those who receive and believe God's prophets.

Jesus the Prophet Was Rejected. While Jesus was ministering on earth as God's true prophet and Messiah He preached and prophesied to the religious leaders of His day. He told them that their fathers had killed the prophets of their time, and now they were building memorials over their tombs to honor them. And He let them know that the greatest prophet of all was among them, yet they were rejecting Him (Lk.11:47-50).

At that time Jesus gave a prophecy that will have its greatest fulfillment during the prophetic and apostolic movements of our generation: "Therefore, also, the wisdom of God said, 'I will send them **prophets** and **apostles** and some of them they will kill and persecute' " (v.49). They declared that they would not have participated in killing the prophets of old, yet they were persecuting and rejecting the one which God had sent among them (Mt.23:27-39). Then he warned, "Woe unto you religious scribes, Pharisees and hypocrites!"

Jesus was prophesying judgment to them because they were continually rejecting and taking away the prophets whom God had established as His key that opens the door to revelation knowledge. As Amos had declared centuries earlier, "Surely the Lord God does nothing unless He reveals His secret counsel to His servants the prophets" (Amos 3:7,NASB; Lk.6:22,23,26).

Then Jesus concluded His prophecy with these words: "Woe to you! For you have taken away the key of knowledge. You did not enter in yourselves, and those who were entering in, you hindered" (Lk.11:52). Thus Jesus declared not only that those who reject God's prophets would be in trouble with God, but also that if such people hindered others from entering into the prophetic ministry they would be further judged. The Prophetic Movement is not to be taken lightly. It is ordained of God, and how people respond to it will affect them greatly. God told prophet Samuel, after Israel said they wanted to have a king like the other nations, that: "They have not rejected thee [the prophet], but they have rejected me [God]" (1Sam.8:6,7,19-22).

The Key to Knowledge. One reason for this book, then, is to help educate the uninformed and the innocent so that they do not sin unknowingly against God and His prophets. I pray that the knowledge found in these pages will help Christians from being hindered from entering into what is being restored in the Church today. Do not allow the "old wineskin" religious leaders who are standing in the door and not going in to hinder you from entering into all that God is doing.

Heroes of the Faith Are Needed Today. There is a desperate need for men and women with the Joshua and Caleb spirit and for modern-day heroes of the faith like those listed in the eleventh chapter of Hebrews. Opportunity does not make heroes, it only reveals them. One person rushes over and pulls the person out of a burning car while others look on in curiosity or horror but do not risk their lives to save another.

Consider, for example, Saul and the Israelite army, who faced the daily challenge from Goliath for forty days. They had an opportunity for heroism yet didn't take it. But when David heard the same challenge from Goliath, he responded with courage and faith in God and was willing to use what he had. He became the hero of the day and saved both his king and the whole army from defeat (1Sam.17:1-58).

Is the Product or Person the Problem? The product can be good and ministered with a proper motive, yet still cause blowouts and breakouts. For instance, true prophecy is the breath of God blowing. It is like putting air into an old inner tube: The air does not make the holes or weak spots; it only reveals them.

In the same way, the infilling of the Holy Spirit within a person or the pouring in of prophetic ministry puts pressure within for power to perform. At the same time, it will manifest any faulty character or weakness in the person's life. It is the build-up of pressure in the steam engine that enables the train to go and the whistle to blow.

The Messenger, the Message or the Ones Receiving? Who is at fault for a church split over new truth: Martin Luther, his "new wine" Protestant teaching or the Catholic church?

The same could be said for those who preached new truth into old wineskin denominations, such as the Baptists with the historic Protestant churches or John Wesley teaching sanctification and perfectionism in historic Protestant churches. The Pentecostal Movement teachings and "tongues talking" experience caused splits and blowouts in hundreds of the old Holiness Movement churches. The Latter Rain ministry of singing praises and personal prophecy caused splits in hundreds of Pentecostal churches.

Jesus made an unalterable and consistent factual statement: You cannot put new wine in an old wineskin or new cloth in an old garment without it ripping apart or bursting. Who is at fault? The person who poured the new wine into the old, dried and set goatskin container; the vessel and the way it responded; or the new wine truth and ministry? (Mt.9:17; Mk.2:22; Lk.5:37).

Holy Ghost Fire Manifests the True Nature. The Apostle Paul's bringing the sticks of wood to the fire did not make one of the sticks turn into a snake. The fire ignited the wood for light and warmth to others, but awakened and activated the viper. A half-frozen snake may look like the other sticks, but when placed in the fire it cannot receive and become a part of the fire. So it resists and reacts by seeking to destroy the man of God who brought it and the fire together (Acts 28:3).

This has been a principle manifested over and over again in every restoration of new truth and ministry. New truth being restored is like rain falling from heaven. Jesus said that He sends the rain and it falls on the just and the unjust. The rain does not make them just or unjust any more than rain makes the seed it causes to sprout into wheat or tares, a fruitful watermelon vine or a poison oak vine (Mt.5:45; Hosea 6:3; Is.55:10).

Should God have been more discreet and timely and waited until all bad seeds were removed from the soil before sending the germinating, life-giving water? You could reason that if there had been proper preparation and purging of the ground of all bad seeds before the rain was sent, it would have prevented the problems of having to deal with bad seed plants.

Can pure water sprout bad seeds? Can true fire awaken snakes? Can truth and life-giving ministry also awaken snakes and activate a bad character or manifestation? The ideal would be to have a pure field with nothing but good seeds for pure water to sprout and grow good fruitful plants.

But Jesus said that the enemy comes during the night and sows bad seeds. Jesus declared there would be tares and wheat growing in the same field (local church or movement) until the time of the great harvest. The Scriptures say, let both grow together until the end time harvest when Jesus the great separator will head up a movement that will separate the tares from among wheat, goats from among sheep and snakes from among sticks. The tares will be gathered and burned, but His wheat will be placed in His Kingdom to reproduce His glory and purpose throughout earth and to the ends of the universe (Mt.13:24-30; 26:32).

The Prophet Prepares the Way for Christ to Return and Put Satan in the Bottomless Pit. A final reminder: This Prophetic Movement has a greater potential for good or evil than any of the previous movements in Church history. The coming forth of the company of prophets is the most ominous sign to the devil that his eternal doom is now at hand. He is now intensifying his activity of going about as a roaring lion seeking whom he may devour (1Pet.5:8; Rev.22:16-20).

Nevertheless, the prophets will prepare the way and make ready a people for the soon return of Jesus Christ. His coming in power and great glory will bring about the cleansing of the heavenlies of all demons and will cast the devil in the bottomless pit. Let us labor with the prophets in preparing the way for the returning of Christ in our generation. *The Spirit and the Bride say, Come. Even so, come, Lord Jesus! Amen.*

The
ETERNAL CHURCH
by DR. BILL HAMON

THE RESTORATION AND
DESTINY OF THE CHURCH

The ETERNAL CHURCH
by Dr. Bill Hamon

IT IS ...
as **factual** as a **textbook**
as **inspiring** as a **devotional**
as **informative** as a **history book**
BUT **reads like** a **novel**

A panoramic view of God's eternal purposes in Church restoration over the past 500 years with special emphasis on the current move of the Holy Spirit and what is next on God's agenda.

REMOVAL or RESTORATION?
More "GROWING UP" before "GOING UP?"
"What is the CHURCH to ACCOMPLISH
ON PLANET EARTH?"

The **Church** portrayed in its **Origination, Deterioration, Restoration** and **Ultimate Destiny.**

Hundreds of prominent Christian leaders have read this book and found it to be worthy of the highest commendation, such as:

John Gimenez, James Beall, Earl Paulk, Jerry Savelle, Gary Greenwald, Ken Sumrall, Paul Billheimer, Kenneth Copeland, Harold Bredesen, and many other **Classical Pentecostal** and **Charismatic leaders.**

Many **pastors** have made the **Eternal Church** required reading for their **leaders** and **saints** and several present-truth Bible **colleges** are using it as a **textbook** in their college classes.

To order your copy of this exciting 400 page book on Church Restoration, see order form in back of book.

Prophets-1

"Prophets and Personal Prophecy"

THERE ARE MORE EXAMPLES OF PERSONAL PROPHECY IN SCRIPTURE THAN ANY OTHER BIBLICAL SUBJECT

GUIDELINES FOR RECEIVING, UNDERSTANDING AND FULFILLING GOD'S PERSONAL WORD TO YOU

Foreword by **Jim Jackson** and also endorsed by **Emanuele Cannistraci, Earl Paulk, Ken Sumrall, Norvel Hayes and Gary Greenwald.** Most prominent Church leaders have read and approved of this work. **50,000 in print.**

"Prophets and Personal Prophecy" is not an abstract theological doctrinal statement but a practical "how to" guide on what personal prophecy is and what you are supposed to do with it. This book is a must for anyone who has ever heard (or even thought they heard) from God."

—**Dr. John Gimenez**

To order your copy of this book on Personal Prophecy, see order form in back.

Prophets-3

Biblical Principles to Practice

and

Personal Pitfalls to Avoid

This volume will be a must for those who plan to press on, with integrity and balance, in the prophetic ministry. Much of what was planned for **Prophets-2** was moved to **Prophets-3** because of the pressing need to make the **Prophetic Movement** known to the Church world.

THE FOLLOWING TOPICS ARE PLANNED TO BE COVERED IN **PROPHETS-3:**

Prophets Calling vs Commissioning
Proper Prophetic Principles to Practice
Prophetic Pitfalls to Avoid
Scriptural Presentations of Various Prophets
Present day Prophets' Calling and Life Experiences
Guidelines for Ministering Personal Prophecy
The 10 M's for Ministering and Maintaining Maturity
Prophets Revealing Restoration Movements
Prophets and Apostles Restorational Relationships
Testimonies of Present day Prophets and Prophetesses
Answers for Pastors on Prophetic Abuses
How Prophets Prophesy Supernatural Knowledge
Developing and Maturing One's Prophetic Perceptions
Ways to Prophesy with Accuracy and Anointing

Prophets-1 gives guidelines for receiving and responding to personal prophecy in many areas of life, but **Prophets-3** will present proper principles for ministering personal prophecy to different people in various situations.

Watch for announcement in CI-NPM Newspaper for release of
Prophets-3.

Christian International
School of Theology

*"Preparation for
Christ's Provision."*

CI's Undergraduate and Graduate School of Theology was founded in 1967 to provide a quality academically sound biblical education through a systematic off-campus study program. CI was one of the first institutions of higher theological education to provide a program for those who could not afford to leave their work or ministry to pursue a traditional on-campus education. Now you can study at your own pace in the privacy of your home and earn a degree in theology.

CI provides a disciplined, organized and thorough curriculum of biblical studies in more than 300 semester hours of courses. Ten major areas of study available from fundamentals of the faith to present truth prophetic ministry. Our educational philosophy can be best stated as *"education without indoctrination, doctrine without dogma."*

We believe **God has established the local church to train,** disciple, raise up, and send out ministries to change the world for Christ. The *Christian International Extension College program* was developed in 1970 to provide the local church with the tools to establish an "in-house" Bible college, for training their own saints and ministers. CI's Extension College Program provides resource materials, curriculum, and over 20 years of expertise to assist local churches in developing their own Bible training center.

Use the card in the back of the book to request complete information packets on CI's Off-Campus and Extension College programs.

NETWORK OF PROPHETIC MINISTRIES

"Providing preparation and place for prophets and prophetic ministry."

The **CI-NPM** is an international association of prophetic ministers founded by Bishop Hamon to provide training, equipping and accountability based on relationship.

The particular purpose of CI-NPM is:

■ to see the **OFFICE OF THE PROPHET FULLY RESTORED** within the Church to the level of acceptance and recognition that the pastor, evangelist and teacher have today.

■ to **TEACH, TRAIN and ACTIVATE** the prophets given to our charge so that they are equipped for **mature, accurate** ministry within the Body of Christ and to the world.

The **SPECIFIC MISSION** God has given us to facilitate these goals are:

■ to be a **CENTRAL HEADQUARTERS** for gathering, uniting, covering and sending forth of **PROPHETIC MINISTERS.**

■ to be a **VITAL RESOURCE CENTER** for books, teaching tapes, workbooks, magazines, videos and other materials needed to propagate the prophetic ministry.

■ to **CONDUCT REGIONAL PROPHETS CONFERENCES** throughout the U.S. and the nations of the world to introduce and take the prophetic ministry into every region of the world.

■ to see the **PROPHETIC PASTORS TRAIN THEIR LEADERSHIP INTO PROPHETIC TEAMS** who minister the gifts and grace of God to edify the Church and to convert the lost by demonstrating the reality of God's love and power.

CI-NPM
Seminars and Ministries

CI SCHOOL OF THE HOLY SPIRIT
Teaching & equipping saints and ministers in the Gifts of the Holy Spirit

CI PROPHETIC MINISTRY SEMINARS
Teaching, training and maturing prophets, prophetic ministers and a prophetic people

CI PROPHETIC BUSINESSMEN'S SEMINARS
Teaching and activating Christian Businessmen to succeed with Biblical principles and prophetic perception

CI WORSHIP & WARFARE SEMINARS
Educating and activating worship and warfare praise leaders

CI PUBLISHERS
Books, tapes, videos and teaching manuals on prophetic ministry and restoration truths of the Church

CI NETWORK OF PROPHETIC MINISTRIES
International association of prophetic ministers providing training and accountability based on relationship

CI PROPHETIC MINISTRY SCHOOL
Three week intensified schooling for prophetic ministry. Promoting proper Pastor and Prophet working relationships